Stencil Style 101

Stencil Style 101

More than 20 Reusable Fashion Stencils with Step-by-Step Project Instructions

Ed Roth
Stencil 1

CHRONICLE BOOKS
SAN FRANCISCO

Library of Congress Cataloging-in-Publication Data available.

ISBN: 978-1-4521-0787-5

Manufactured in China
Designed by TO/GO/TK

Models: Carlo Romero, Lucia Martinez

Converse All Star Chuck Taylor is a registered trademark of Converse Inc. Flashe is a registered trademark of Societe Des Couleurs Lefranc & Bourgeois Corp. Hermès is a registered trademark of Hermès International. Lycra is a registered trademark of Invista North American S.A.R.L. Corp. Martha Stewart Crafts is a registered trademark of Martha Stewart Living Omnimedia, Inc. MUJI is a registered trademark of Ryohin Keikaku Co., Ltd. Mylar is a registered trademark of E.I. Du Pont de Nemours and Company Corp. NIKEiD is a registered trademark of Nike, Inc. Stained by Sharpie is a registered trademark of Sanford. Stencil1 is a registered trademark of Stencil1, Inc. UGG is a registered trademark of Deckers Outdoor Corp. X-Acto is a registered trademark of Elmer's Products, Inc.

Please use caution when doing any craft project. Situations and conditions may vary, so always use your common sense. Check product labels to be sure that the materials are safe and nontoxic and take care to use them according to the manufacturer's instructions and safety warnings. The author and publisher disclaim all liability from any damage or injury that may result from the directions or information in this book, whether used properly or improperly. Although creativity in stenciling your own property is a good thing, you should respect the property rights of others, including public agencies and offices. Stencil responsibly!

10 9 8 7 6 5 4 3 2 1

Chronicle Books LLC
680 Second Street
San Francisco, California 94107
www.chroniclebooks.com

CONTENTS

Visit www.chroniclebooks.com/stencilstyle for
three bonus projects!

5

INTRODUCTION

Everyone has their own unique style.

The New York City subway is often crowded and cramped, and at times smelly. But I love the opportunity to people-watch. In this underground melting pot, you can easily spot the latest trends— on the Condé Nast girls with their towering heels and huge bags, thuggy boys with their pant waists around their knees, or hipsters slouching in their skinny-jean uniforms. Everyone has their own unique take on style.

One of my biggest inspirations in fashion spotting is the unassum-ing street photographer Bill Cunningham, who shoots for the *New York Times*. Mr. Cunningham rides around the city on his bicycle, taking pictures of anything he considers fashionable and beautiful. He is not interested in the fashion shows; he enjoys the "show on the street" and gravitates toward fashionistas who express their individualism via their own styling, rather than those who pay others to do it for them. In the 2010 documentary *Bill Cunningham New York*, he says that we are all blank canvases, and we paint ourselves.

DIY fashion has grown out of that craving for individuality. It's one thing to be "in style," but who wants to wear the same thing as the guy or gal next to them? And how cool is it to say, "I made this!"? Major brands, like Nike and Vans, have responded to this desire for individuality by offering online customization of their wares. Well, why not take it further and get tactile? You can do the customizing yourself.

I created *Stencil Style 101* to give you tools and inspiration to create your own unique look. In this book, you will find twenty stencils—from animal prints to bold icons—geared specifically toward customizing apparel. Plus, my guest artists and I show you numerous techniques to create some pretty impressive looks. We don't just cover making T-shirts— we delve into advanced techniques, like embroidery, appliqué, and more.

In the summer of 2011, I had the pleasure of attending the Alexander McQueen exhibit at the Metropolitan Museum of Art. This master designer left us a legacy of inspiration beyond imagination. His use of metal-working, appliqué, and embroidery is mind-blowing, incorporating razor clamshells, glass, or millions of tiny bugle beads into sculptural garments that evoke wonder, discomfort, and awe.

A dress of crimson chrysanthemum-shaped roundels embroidered onto a nude silk gown took my breath away. These small floral "patches" were not that extraordinary individually, but once they were applied to the gown, the combination was stunning— a reminder that something seemingly small or mundane can be miraculous.

My point is: Use this little book to DREAM BIG. You can make a tiny stencil image into a marvelous piece of art!

You can use Stencil1 stencils to upcycle countless apparel combinations from the thrift store or the back of your closet. Most of the clothes you see in this book came from vintage or recycled-clothing stores in my neighborhood, some for pocket change. You can also use these stencils on walls, furniture—whatever you can paint. So dive in and create that one-of-a-kind garment or, as Little Edie Beale would say, "the best costume for the day."

—Ed Roth

MATERIALS

Everything You Need to Know to Get Started

All materials recommended in this book can be found at your local hardware store, art supply store, or fabric store.

STENCILS

Card-stock stencils are reusable, at least for several uses. To extend the life of your card-stock stencils, wipe excess paint from the stencil after use—especially around the edges—with a slightly damp cloth or paper towel. Allow them to dry flat and store them in a dry, flat place. Flip to the back of the book for 20 stencils to choose from. You can find more stencils at www.stencil1.com and in my other Chronicle Books publications: *Stencil 101*, *Stencil 201*, and *Stencil 101 Decor*. Or design and cut your own (see How to Make Your Own Stencils on page 9).

BRUSHES & ROLLERS

Stencil brushes

Stencil brushes are different from standard paintbrushes in that they have a round, flat bristle head and are a little stiffer, to allow stencil pouncing. Pouncing is basically a technique in which you tap the paint onto the stencil, rather than brushing it on. The brushes come in a variety of diameters; I recommend any size between ¼ in/6 mm and 1½ in/4 cm.

Foam brushes

These affordable brushes, usually made of gray foam with a wood handle, are great for small stencil projects. They can be discarded after use. Newer designs, called pouncers (or spouncers), have a dome-shaped head and are better for stenciling than the rectangular ones, especially if you want to use the pouncing technique. They cost more but are also more versatile.

ADHESIVES

Repositionable spray adhesive

This adhesive is used to hold your stencil securely in place while you are stenciling your design. You'll apply it lightly to the back of the stencil, allow it to dry until it is tacky, and then attach the stencil to the surface you are painting.

Note: While you're at it, buy some spray adhesive remover, a citrus-based cleanser. It will extend the life of your stencils!

Blue painter's tape

Use this tape for holding your stencil in place. It won't damage your surface, and it works beautifully. Any other type of tape will pull the existing paint off your surface or leave an oily stain.

CUTTING TOOLS
(IF MAKING YOUR OWN STENCILS)

Utility knife with #11 blades and/or an electric stencil cutter or burner

You will also need a rubber or glass cutting board if attempting to cut your own stencils.

Scissors

Any type of crafting shears will be fine for the projects in this book.

PAINTS, INKS & OTHER PIGMENTS

Depending on your project, choose the paint appropriate for the surface you are painting. See the list below for suggestions or consult with your paint supply store to choose the right paint for your project.

SURFACE	PAINT TYPE
CANVAS	Acrylic, fabric paint, Stencil1 Sprayers, or spray paints (Be aware that oil paints are much less forgiving and messier than acrylics. These are better for professional usage.)
FABRIC	Fabric paint, Stencil1 Sprayer, or acrylic paint with fabric medium (acrylic polymer emulsion) mixed at 1:1 ratio
WOOD	Acrylic or oil paint (Your design must be glaze-coated after stenciling, to protect the design.)
SUEDE, LEATHER	Water-based acrylic paint designed for leather, leather paint, or spray paint (with mixed results)

MISCELLANEOUS MATERIALS

Bleach paste pen
A bleach paste pen contains a thick, easy-to-control paste that's perfect for stenciling.

Cardboard boxes or sheets
Place boxes or sheets of cardboard between fabrics (T-shirts and coats, for example) to prevent paint from seeping through to the next layer. Sheets or boxes should just fit inside the fabric, not stretched so much that it could distort your design.

Iron
Heat sealing with an iron ensures paint projects will stand up to the wash and everyday wear.

Newspaper or butcher paper
Protect your work surface by covering it with newspaper or butcher paper.

Paint palettes
A saucer, plate, plastic egg carton, or artist's palette—any of these will do for holding and mixing your paints.

Paper towels
These are essential for cleanup.

Puff paint
While this is a paint, it can also be used to secure gems to sweaters!

Ruler or Straightedge
A ruler or straightedge is used for perfecting a design on your surface and is ideal for patterns on apparel with even, consistent measurements.

Sandpaper
To prepare surfaces for painting, such as to smooth leather.

Scrap cardboard or thick paper
Use to avoid overspray. Cover the outer edges of the stencil with paper or cardboard and tape, so as to not paint outside the edges of your stencil.

T-shirts
Paint and bleach love 100 percent cotton T-shirts. You can use standard cotton T-shirts, like Hanes or Fruit of the Loom, or get an array of colors and cuts by American Apparel or Alternative Apparel.

PROJECT-SPECIFIC MATERIALS

- American cowhide leather
- Anti-Chlor, Bleach Stop, or any bleach neutralizer
- Bowl
- Card stock, thin acetate, or transparency sheets
- Clear polyurethane sealant spray
- Canvas sneakers or slip-ons
- Cloth tote bag
- Clothespins or binder clips
- Colorful sweater or sweatshirt
- Cotton ball or small rag
- Cotton or wool tie
- Craft glue
- Damp cloth
- Denim jacket
- Embroidery floss or crewel yarn
- Embroidery hoop
- Fabric glue
- Fabric markers
- Felting needle
- Foam block for needle felting
- Fusible web or iron-on interfacing
- Goggles
- Glitter
- Grommet kit and pyramid studs
- Hair dryer
- Helmet
- Hooded sweatshirt
- Insulated jacket
- Iron
- Knitting chart paper
- Knitting needles
- Leather apparel or accessory
- Leather or suede boots
- Leather suitcase
- Messenger cap
- Paper plate or tray
- Pencil
- Photoshop or comparable photo-editing computer program
- Printer or print facility
- Rubber gloves
- Rubber or glass cutting board
- Rubbing alcohol or acetone
- Sequins, beads, pearls, gems, studs, or beetle wings (you'll understand!)
- Sewing machine
- Sewing machine that can handle leather, ideally with a walking foot
- Sewing and embroidery needles
- Sidney & Sons canvas bag
- Solid-colored cotton fabric
- Solid-colored dog T-shirt
- Solid-colored silk scarf
- Stained by Sharpie Fabric Markers
- Stiff wire brush
- Stitch markers
- Suit jacket or sport coat
- Tailor's chalk
- Tank top (or garment of your choice)
- Thread
- Thick canvas
- Washtub or large pot
- Wood bangles
- Wool baby sweater
- Wool coat
- Wool felt
- Wool roving
- Yarn
- Yarn needle

HOW TO MAKE YOUR OWN STENCILS

There are several ways to design your own stencils. You can draw your own designs on the stencil material itself, or you can design something on the computer and print it out.

Hand-drawing your own stencil designs

Materials needed:
Thin acetate or transparency sheets
Pencil
Black marker
Rubber or glass cutting board
Utility knife and #11 blades
Electric stencil cutter or burner
   (optional)

Hand-drawing your stencil designs is a great way to get started in stencil making before jumping into more complicated, computer-generated designs. Stencils are made up of various cutout shapes, called "islands." The spaces between these shapes are called "bridges." When you draw your design, you want the bridges to be strong; otherwise, the stencil will rip easily.

Take, for example, our simple star pattern below. On the left, the dark areas between the light cutout shapes are too thin and will rip or tear. The design on the right shows those areas made wider and therefore stronger. Keep this in mind as you draw your designs.

For instance, if you were creating a heart stencil, you'd trace the shape onto your stencil material and then fill in the heart shape with black marker to indicate the area to be cut out. Keep in mind that the white areas will have to connect with bridges. Otherwise, when the stencil is cut, the unconnected areas, or islands, will simply fall out. Bridges are what hold the stencil together, so you have to create bridges to the island. A simple example of this is the letter e, which has a hollow area known in typography circles as a "counter." If you were to cut out your letter e to make a stencil, you also would be cutting away the island, or counter. To remedy this, you have to create a bridge to the island with black pen (see the diagram below). The wider you make your bridge, the stronger your stencil will be.

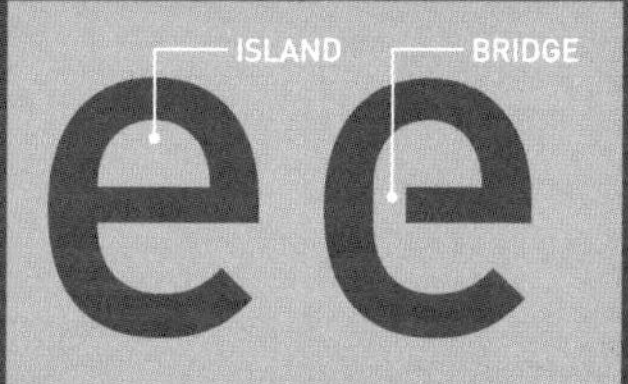

To start, choose a pattern and draw or trace it on transparency film, acetate, or card stock using a black marker with a pointed tip. Fill in the design's open shapes with black marker. Everything black will be the cutaway portion of the stencil. Once you've completed filling in the areas to be cut out, you'll cut out your stencil.

Designing stencils on the computer

Materials needed:
Photoshop or comparable
   photo-editing computer
   program
Printer or print facility
Transparency sheets, thin acetate,
   or card stock
Utility knife and #11 blades
Rubber or glass cutting board
Electric stencil cutter or burner
   (optional)

If you want to make an image for your stencil on your computer, the first step is to plan out your design. It pays to think ahead here. First, consider the size of your stencil. This is usually determined by where you will be applying the image: a specific wall or a certain area on a T-shirt, for example. Next, draw your image or select a source image. If working from a source image, first make sure you have the rights to use it if you plan on distributing it. Next, choose an image with detail and contrast, not a blurry or overexposed photo. If you are planning on making a small stencil, you will probably want to choose a less detailed image. Cutting out intricate detail is very difficult by hand.

TIP: Don't feel you have to use the exact details of the photo. Say, for example, you are making a stencil of a skull. When you search around for images, maybe you like the eye sockets on one photo, the nose detail on another, the teeth on another. In the photo editor, you can combine these features into one new, perfected image and then work from that "Frankensteined" photo. I am getting ahead of myself, but it's something to consider at this stage of the game.

Once you've settled on your design, bring your final reference image into your photo editor.

Size your design to the exact size you want the stenciled image to be (click Image, then Image size, then enter new dimensions in the document size boxes). Print out the resized image to be certain the size is correct.

Convert your image to grayscale (click Image, Mode, Grayscale). Duplicate the layer, name it "Reference," and shut it off. This is so you can always refer back if needed. Select your main layer again to work on.

Paint away the detail of the photo you are not using in the stencil design. Select the paintbrush tool, select white as the color you are painting with, and adjust your brush size to a size that's easy to work with. For example, if you are doing a stencil from a photo of someone's face, you can paint white all of the photo's background detail, his or her neck and shirt, etc. You should also paint in details that you feel will disappear when you contrast the image in the next steps.

Next, play with brightness and contrast to give it the "stencil look" (click Image, Adjustments, Brightness/Contrast). Start by adjusting the contrast to 100 percent. Now, adjust the brightness until you get more of a contrasted stencil appearance. Not looking like a stencil? Maybe your photo was too low-contrast or grainy. Another, sometimes better, way is to adjust levels (click Image, Adjustments, Levels), then slide your black, white, and gray input levels until you have a stencil look.

Now, here is the tricky part: Just because it looks like a stencil doesn't mean it will cut right. You now have to create the bridges and eliminate the islands (see previous section). As with hand-drawing stencils, the islands have to be eliminated on the computer. You can do this two ways: Use the paintbrush tool to draw in bridges that create "peninsulas," or fill in the islands with black, meaning they, too, will be part of the design that is cut away.

Here is how we typically draw an eye:

If you cut out all the black areas, the eye shape would just be one hollow shape and the detail would cut away as well, so . . .

Here is the eye with bridges:

And remember, you are making stencil art. Feel free to draw free-hand areas into your design that you could not cut into the stencil. For example, add some white dots in the eyes to give the eye some life. You are an artist, not just a stencil artist!

So create all the bridges you need throughout the image to eliminate the islands. Make the bridges thick enough that they won't tear.

Next, print your design. If you have a laser printer, you can print directly onto transparency or acetate sheets; just make sure that your print medium is compatible with the printer (check the packaging). If you do not have compatible paper, no worries—you can print on card stock (heavyweight paper), then cut the acetate on top of this print. If you do not have a printer, go to the local print facility and have them print it for you.

Cutting

Now, time to cut it out! A utility knife with a #11 blade is the weapon of choice. Here's a tip: Make your life easier and change the blade often. Wait, did you hear me? Change the blade often. It gets dull fast! Do all of your cutting on a rubber cutting board or a thick glass cutting board with a smooth surface. Some swear by cutting on glass, as it has more resistance than the rubber boards and makes the cutting go faster. See what works for you.

Tape the acetate to your printed image so it doesn't slip around while cutting, and place both sheets on the cutting board. Starting with the smallest, inner-most point of the design, cut out the black areas. The more you cut away, the weaker the sheet becomes, so be cautious and take your time. If you rip a bridge, press on—you can always tape it back together and trim any excess tape away. You will find your most comfortable way of cutting; some like to move or rotate the entire sheet, rather than trying to cut curves with just the blade movement. Depending on the complexity of the design, this could take minutes—or it could take an evening or two! This step just takes practice.

TIP: If you own an electric stencil cutter or burner, you should trace the stencil design onto the acetate, then cut it out with glass board below. These heated knives cut through transparency sheets and acetate like *butta*, but you don't want paper or rubber involved with the heated knife!

You can also send Stencil1 your art for custom laser cutting in any size: www.stencil1.com/quote.php. Once you have cut out the design, you can remove the printed backing. Your reusable stencil is ready to use!

TECHNIQUES

Basic and Advanced Moves!

Stenciling is different from traditional ways of painting—from the brushes and the preparation to the motion of painting itself. Here is a guide to the basics of stenciling, along with advanced techniques you can try.

The Basics

Let's start with the most basic of tools. The brush you use should be a round, flat-headed stencil brush with firm bristles. Sizes vary from ¼ in/6 mm in diameter to 2 in/ 5 cm in diameter across the bristle head. Choose your brush size based on the size of the open areas in the stencil you are using. In other words, for small, detailed stencils, you will want to use a small, ¼- to ½-in/6- to 12-mm brush, while for large, pattern stencils, a 2-in/5-cm brush will be more efficient.

Since kindergarten, we have painted by dipping a brush into the paint jar and then going right to our paper (or wall or cat) with that loaded brush. Not so with stenciling, which requires a dry-brush technique. To dry-brush, dip your brush in a small amount of paint. Now, before painting in the stenciled areas, "dry" off the brush by dabbing some of the paint onto a plate or a paper towel. You need very little paint to fill in the open areas of a stencil, and using too much will cause paint to seep under the edges of your stencil.

Now you have your appropriately sized brush loaded with just the right amount of paint, and you're itching to apply it. Let's talk about motion. The goal of stenciling is crisp, clean edges. The most effective painting method is an up-and-down "pouncing" motion, dabbing the paint until the open areas of the design are filled in. You want to avoid the classic paint-brushing motion of sweeping paint across a surface. Talk about seepage! With large open stencil areas, you may want to use brushstrokes in the center of the open areas and then pounce around the edges. This combination of techniques will speed things along and still give you crisp edges.

Ohh, that's shady!

A nice way to create some depth in your design is to shade in the stencil areas. Rather than have one even amount of color across your design, you can darken the edges of the open design areas. First, lightly pounce in all the open areas with color. Then, from the outside edge of the open area moving inward, brush in more color. Finally, starting on the solid area of stencil, brush inward across all the edges of the open areas. This trick makes your work look more labor-intensive and creates depth.

A kind gesture . . .

Remember, a stencil is really just a guide to help you draw or paint the image or pattern you see. You may think you should fill all the cutout shapes to do it "right," but this trick will let you be more expressive, especially with bold pattern designs such as those found in *Stencil 101 Decor*. Rather than a pouncing motion, use regular paint strokes to paint in the open shapes, working in the direction they are shaped. This technique reminds me of sumi-e painting, the Japanese art of painting black ink on white paper. The end result gives a more painterly or hand-drawn look. I think it's particularly effective on apparel, as I have spotted so many painterly patterns on the street.

Stencil within a stencil

Again, stencils don't always have to be filled in with solid fields of color. By layering a small, repeating stencil over a larger stencil with very bold cutouts, you get a textural, shape-within-a-shape effect. Imagine you want to paint on a T-shirt a large open stencil of the number 1. You lay the 1 on the shirt, and then lay a stencil of hundreds of tiny stars on top of the 1 stencil. Once you paint, you will have a 1 made up of hundreds of little stars! And you don't have to use a stencil for the top layer—you can lay a piece of lace, a window screen, mesh, etc. Get experimental.

Aged beauty

Everyone loves the age and softness of a cool vintage shirt. Well, shirts are now being produced to have that vintage look without requiring all those years of "earning it." There are stenciling tricks that allow you to achieve this look for yourself. First, do not fill in all the areas of the design or apply the paint evenly—go heavy in some areas and light in others. If tiling a pattern on a shirt, you may leave out sections of the pattern, giving a dissipating look to the overall print. Or, once you've stenciled, you can rub, drag, or smear the paint, or even wash off areas of the design. Oh, and make sure you use a super-soft shirt!

Street Style

Get street smart and give your projects a more graffiti-inspired aesthetic by adding sprays, drips, and blotches. You can spray clothes using Stencil1 Sprayers, and for some extra drips, just unscrew the spray nozzle and tap some excess paint off the nozzle straw, much the way someone would ash a cigarette. If you want running drips on leather, use spray paint generously on a vertical surface until it runs. This is experimental so get into it! And when you stencil, don't mask the other areas with paper for the oversprayed look!

How-to Projects

The Classic Stencil1 T-Shirt

Paint One- and Two-Layer Stencils

OVERVIEW

Ah, the graphic tee. Is it ever out of style? Consider all these options: You can stencil your T-shirt with one big image, with a repeating pattern, in high-contrast colors, or with a subtle tone-on-tone palette. With all these choices, you are sure to create a one-of-a-kind piece of wearable art.

I will mention two techniques. The first uses fabric paint and a stencil brush; the second uses Stencil1 Sprayers, our multi-surface spray ink, for a more spray-painted, graffiti-esque look. We will cover one- and two-layer stencils.

MATERIALS

- ✿ **T-shirt**
- ✿ **Fabric cream paint** or **Stencil1 Sprayers**
- ✿ **Cardboard, shipping box,** or **shirt box**
- ✿ **Stencil(s)**
- ✿ **Stencil spray adhesive** or **pushpins**
- ✿ **Blue painter's tape** (if using 2 stencils)
- ✿ **Stencil brushes, foam brushes,** or **pouncer foam brushes**
- ✿ **Safety goggles** (if spray-painting)
- ✿ **Thick paper, cardboard,** or **poster board to control overspray** (if spray-painting)
- ✿ **Iron** or **hair dryer**

INSTRUCTIONS

1. Choose your T-shirt

Prewashed or preshrunk, 100 percent cotton T-shirts work best. Polyester blends (50/50) yield mixed results, since they don't absorb the paint well. It is best to experiment first or to avoid them.

2. Choose your fabric paint

You'll find fabric paints at art supply stores. They require no mixing, have a thick consistency, are rich in pigmentation, and give long-lasting results. They even stand up to washing and drying. You can also use acrylic paint mixed with fabric medium (also available at art or craft supply stores) in a 1:1 ratio. Make sure the mixture is well blended. Stencil1 also has a line of multi-surface sprays. Stencil1 Sprayers are ideal for fabric. For a rougher look, you can use traditional spray paint, but with no guaranteed results. For a more advanced application, try an airbrush kit. These are available at many art supply stores, and when you use them with fabric paint, you'll get fantastic results. If you are using a two-layer stencil, choose a color for the silhouette layer (the first layer) and another (usually, but not always, darker) color for the second, more detailed layer.

3. Prepare your T-shirt

Stretch your T-shirt over a piece of rectangular cardboard, a shipping box, or a shirt box to prevent paint from seeping through to the back of the T-shirt. This will also provide a flat surface to paint on.

[CONT.]

RING
MY
BELL

Make sure you don't stretch the shirt too much, or your design will be "warped" once you take it off the box. Tip: Is your shirt too big for the box? Just bind the excess fabric in the back with a rubber band to make the front side of the shirt lie flat.

4. Position the stencil

One-Layer Stencil
Place the stencil on the shirt where you'd like the image to appear. Secure the stencil firmly in place using spray adhesive or pushpins. If you use spray adhesive, apply a light layer to the back of the stencil. Allow the adhesive to dry until the surface becomes tacky, and then position your stencil.

Two-Layer Stencil
Position the silhouette stencil, and be sure to stick four very small pieces of blue tape on the shirt under the stencil's triangular registration marks. You will use these marks later to align your second-layer stencil. Now, secure the stencil firmly in place, using either spray adhesive or pushpins. Draw in the triangular registration marks on the blue tape with a pen. The tape allows you to make your registration marks without marking on the T-shirt and keeps you from accidentally painting in those triangles when stenciling. Tip: I use registration marking when I make T-shirts—I just eyeball it!

5. Start painting

You can use stencil brushes, foam brushes, or Stencil1 Sprayers to apply paint. If using a brush, do not overload it with paint. Too much paint on the brush causes the paint to seep under the edges of the stencil and creates blotchy designs. Remember, stenciling is a dry-brush technique. The most common mistake is overloading your brush. It is far better to build up the color gradually, layer by layer, instead of using one thick paint application. If paint begins to seep behind your stencil or if your designs do not have crisp, defined edges, you may be using too much paint.

Simply tap or dab the loaded brush against the stencil openings. I recommend practicing on paper before you begin on your T-shirt. If you're using any kind of spray paint, be sure to wear safety goggles and cover the outer edges of the stencil and your T-shirt with thick paper, so as to not spray outside the stencil. Then, spray several small, light sprays in the open areas of the stencil. Once all areas are filled, carefully remove the stencil from the shirt to see your design. Be careful to lift the stencil parallel to your tee, so as not to let excess paint drip on your shirt. Tip: If paint does drip, add more drips all around the design for an oversprayed look that's very '80s.

To achieve a tone-on-tone effect, choose a paint color that is just a shade lighter or darker than your shirt color.

6. Seal it

Heat press your T-shirt before finishing or going on to the second stencil. After the paint has dried, turn the shirt inside out and iron the painted area on high heat for 1 to 2 minutes. You can also blow-dry with a hair dryer for 1 to 2 minutes. If you are using a two-layer stencil, proceed to Step 7. You can skip to Step 8 if you used a one-layer stencil.

Two-Layer Stencil
7. Position the second stencil

Prep the shirt as you did in Step 3. Position the second stencil over the area you already painted. Line up the second-layer registration marks with the first-layer marks you made for a perfectly layered design, or just eyeball it. For a real DIY look, you can offset the second layer. If you used tape, remove it before heat sealing.

8. Paint and seal

Repeat Step 5 with the detailed stencil. Let the paint dry and repeat Step 6 to heat seal your new two-layered design. Your T-shirt is ready to wear.

9. Repeat and create

For an all-over pattern, keep moving your stencil and repeat Steps 4, 5, and 6 as many times as you desire.

10. Clean up

Lay your stencil flat to dry, wiping off any heavy paint. Careful cleaning and drying of your stencil brushes will enable them to be used again and again. Wash all excess paint off the brushes with warm running water and soap. Dry the brushes thoroughly before reuse.

15

EV
OL
VE

White Out

Bleach Stencil a T-Shirt

Guest Artist: Clark Clark

OVERVIEW

Clean up your act! Power wash is the art of stenciling on grimy walls and sidewalks, in which you lay down a stencil and wash away the open design areas with a power hose. Essentially, you are "cleaning away" the design.

I first saw this technique in Vieques, Puerto Rico, where Jose Trelles installs antiwar stencil imagery. He applied images of army trucks and helicopters breaking open to reveal butterflies and doves on the walls of U.S. Navy bomb shelters—a protest statement with a lot of strength.

Bleach stenciling is an apparel technique inspired by power washing.

Clark Clark designed the VOTE stencil for Barack Obama's 2008 presidential campaign and designed the EVOLVE stencil in this book,

which is very cool in my opinion. Here's what he said about the design:

"*Evolve is a one-word manifesto for my art. I never want to be stagnant, so my art is constantly evolving and adapting to my surroundings, whether it be the community in which I live or the news of the day. Evolution is about diversity, and I am always working on a variety of projects at any given time.*

My art is also about adapting other artists' ideas, evolving their work to make it my own. It is in itself an evolution of Robert Indiana's art.

Evolve is a call to action to those who read it—a reminder to never become stuck or too set in their ways."

INSTRUCTIONS

1. Choose your T-shirt

The T-shirt should be 100 percent cotton and a darker color for the best results. Start by inserting a cardboard box inside the T-shirt. This flattens the area you want to stencil and prevents the bleach from seeping through to the next layer. The T-shirt should not be too stretched over the cardboard; it should just fit. If you overstretch your fabric, your design will get distorted.

2. Position the stencil

Carefully position the stencil on the shirt where you would like it to appear. Next, secure two or three sides of the stencil with pushpins, masking tape, or spray adhesive to hold your stencil in place. If you use spray adhesive, apply a light layer to the back of the stencil. Allow the adhesive to dry until the surface becomes tacky, and then position your stencil.

3. Start painting

Wearing goggles and rubber gloves, squeeze a few blobs of bleach paste out of the pen and into the painting dish or bowl. Dip the foam or stencil brush in the bleach and dab it onto the clothing in the open areas of the stencil, starting with the larger areas.

For a clearer design, try not to get any paste under the stencil. Apply evenly to all areas of the design.

4. Wait

You may start to see the bleach lifting the color out of the shirt immediately. You can leave the paste on for 5 minutes to 4 hours, depending on the effect you want. The longer you leave on the bleach, the more it will lift out the original color of the clothing, so results will vary. But beware! Bleach will eat holes in the shirt if left on too long.

5. Rinse

Prepare a bath of Anti-Chlor, Bleach Stop, or another bleach neutralizer in the washtub. Once you like the look of your design, rinse the T-shirt in water and plunge it into the bleach neutralizer bath. Launder the garment as usual.

6. Take it further

Here's a bonus idea: Try painting an additional layer on top of your bleached design for more depth. See Project 1: Two-Layer Stencil for tips on how to layer a painted design over your bleached design.

7. Clean up

Careful cleaning and drying of your stencils will allow you to use them again and again. Wipe any excess bleach off your stencil with a damp cloth and pat dry with paper towels.

MATERIALS

- Dark-colored T-shirt
- Cardboard shipping box, or shirt box
- Stencil
- Pushpins, masking tape, or spray adhesive
- Goggles*
- Rubber gloves*
- Bleach paste pen*
- Painting dish or bowl
- Foam brush or stencil brush
- Anti-Chlor, Bleach Stop, or any bleach neutralizer
- Washtub or large pot
- Paper towels

*Always wear safety goggles and gloves when working with bleach. The bleach pen is filled with a bleach paste, as opposed to liquid bleach, which allows control of the bleach and keeps it from bleeding too far out of the design areas. For even greater control, I recommend using a small foam brush.

Woolly Embroidery

Stitch a Wool Coat

OVERVIEW

Embroidery is the art of embellishing fabric using a needle and thread or yarn. Embroidery may also incorporate metal, pearls, beads, quills, and sequins. The only limit is your imagination.

In June 2011, I attended the Alexander McQueen exhibit at the Metropolitan Museum of Art. If you want to marvel at technique and be completely inspired by the art of fashion, check out his collections and the book *Alexander McQueen: Savage Beauty*. The embroidery was like none I have ever seen!

Inspired by McQueen's work, this tutorial shows you how to embroider a wool coat to make it uniquely your own. Whether you're a beginner or advanced stitcher, you can create embroidered finery worthy of a fashionista.

MATERIALS

- Wool coat
- Stencil
- Masking tape
- Pencil, washable ink pen, or tailor's chalk
- Embroidery hoop
- Small, sharp scissors
- Embroidery floss or crewel yarn
- Sewing needle (sharp, medium-size)
- Beads, pearls, or other embellishments*

*optional

INSTRUCTIONS

1. Prep the fabric

Lay your coat on a hard, smooth surface. Then place the stencil on the area of fabric that you want to stitch, smoothing out any wrinkles in the fabric. Secure the stencil in place with masking tape.

2. Trace the stencil

Follow the lines of the stencil with a pencil or washable ink pen. (If you're stenciling on a dark fabric, you can use sharpened tailor's chalk instead.) Remove the stencil to reveal the design.

3. Get ready to stitch

Place an embroidery hoop around the design to tighten the fabric. With the scissors, cut a length of embroidery floss or crewel yarn about 12 in/30.5 cm long (roughly the distance from your thumb and forefinger to your elbow). Thread the needle, and make a knot at the tail end so the floss won't pull through the fabric (no need to make a knot at the needle end; just pull it through enough that it won't slip through the eye while you're working).

4. Stitch that stencil (design)

Start by outlining the stencil design with embroidery stitches. Begin from behind the fabric, not by going through the front. Bring your needle up from under the fabric along a chosen starting point in the design—anywhere can be the "beginning." Tip: It's best to work in sections, rather than thinking of the whole design when choosing a starting point. Now, bring the needle back down through the front of the fabric about ¼ in/6 mm from where you came up. You've made a stitch! A little less than ¼ in/6 mm is a good length for your stitches.

5. Do the backstitch

To continue along the line of the design in a "backstitch," bring your needle up along the pattern line, but a space ahead of the end of your last stitch. Now, reinsert your needle through the front of the fabric in the same exit point (going "back") as the end of your last stitch. Pull through, and close the gap. Repeat. Continue along the line of the design until you hit the knot or reach the tail end (holding the tail in place). Other easy, fun outline stitches are stem stitch and split stitch; you can find lots of directions and how-tos online.

6. Jump-skip

There are two ways to move to a new section: You can tie off your floss to keep things neat, or you can make a "jump stitch" by skipping to a new section along the underside of the fabric. Jump stitches should be avoided if they'll show though the front of your fabric or if they're too long. You can also tie off if you'd like to change colors before moving on. It's up to you!

7. Rethread, repeat

When you come to the end of a strand of floss, you can tie it off just by making a plain old knot or by weaving the remaining floss (the "tail") along the underside of the stitches. Cut a new length of floss, rethread that needle, and keep going. Repeat until you have covered the stencil line with stitches.

8. Take it further

If you are a more advanced embroiderer, play around with different outline and fill stitches, like a chain or satin stitch. Or try combining painting and stitching techniques. Follow the painted T-shirt project instructions on page 13, outlining the heat-sealed design with stitching for an awesome, 3-D effect. You can also McQueen your design by threading beads, pearls, wire, or sequins onto your floss and stitching them onto your coat for a couture look of your own.

Patch Work

Paint Rock 'n' Roll Patches

OVERVIEW

As a teenager, I would jump on the bus to New York City from my small hometown in New Jersey and head into Greenwich Village to go shopping. I'd hit up Unique Antique Boutique, Flip, and all the small record stores. I'd buy band pins, rubber bracelets, vinyl records, and canvas band patches to sew onto my jacket or backpack. They were always off-white canvas and black ink. This how-to pays homage to that classic punk trend.

MATERIALS

- ⬡ **Thick canvas**
- ⬡ **Iron**
- ⬡ **Needle and thread**
- ⬡ **Sewing machine***
- ⬡ **Stencil**
- ⬡ **Blue painter's tape** or **spray adhesive**
- ⬡ **Stencil brush**
- ⬡ **Black fabric paint in jar**
- ⬡ **Plate** or **paper towels**

***optional**

Note: Stenciling canvas is very easy, since this material is a cinch to paint. But first you need to make the patches! You can find premade blank patches online at www.stitchalogo.com/index.html or make your own. To DIY, buy 1 yd/1 m or less of thick, off-white canvas from an art supply store.

INSTRUCTIONS

1. Prep it

Cut out the desired size patch from the canvas and iron the fabric. (This will assure that the stencil lies nice and flat and will make it easier to sew.) By hand with the needle and thread or with a sewing machine, stitch the edges of your cutout with a zigzag backstitch. This will protect your canvas patch from unraveling at the edges. Your patch is ready to paint!

2. Set it

Now, place your stencil on the patch where you'd like your image to appear. Use blue painter's tape to secure it in place. Alternatively, you can spray the back of the stencil with adhesive, let dry for 30 to 60 seconds, and adhere to your canvas patch.

3. Paint it

Using your stencil brush, dip the brush lightly in the paint, then dab most of the paint off on a plate or paper towel. With an up-and-down motion, fill in the open areas of the stencil. A swirling motion will help you get into the smaller areas of the design.

4. Check it

Lift the stencil when satisfied, and let dry. Turn the patch over and iron the printed area on high heat for 1 to 2 minutes.

5. Clean it

Wipe your stencil off with a slightly damp cloth and allow it to dry flat. Wash all excess paint off the brushes with warm running water and soap. Dry the brushes thoroughly before reuse.

6. Live it

Sew your patches anywhere you feel they will get the most attention!

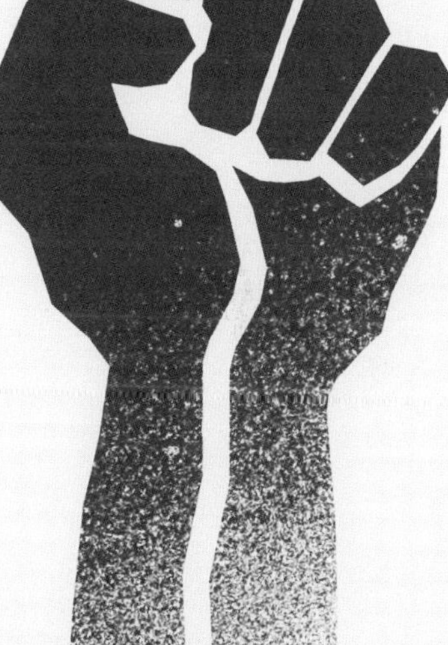

Custom Kicks

Personalize Sneakers with Stained by Sharpie Fabric Markers

OVERVIEW

Back in the day, I customized my Chucks with paint and Sharpies. Now, you can customize your footwear online, via NIKEiD, Vans, and Converse. These apps are cool, but it's way more fun when you get your hands dirty. This tutorial shows you how to customize your kicks the old-fashioned way! Plus, you'll have endless color choices and be able to step out and say, "I made them."

MATERIALS

○ Canvas sneakers or slip-ons
○ Stencil
○ Spray adhesive
○ Stained by Sharpie Fabric Markers
○ Hair dryer

INSTRUCTIONS

1. Choose your sneakers

A canvas sneaker or slip-on works best for this project. If you want to paint leather sneakers, you can use acrylic paint, as long as the label says the paint can be used on leather. Check out Project 17: These Boots Were Made for Walkin'—Customize Leather or Suede Boots for step-by-step instructions on that method.

2. Prep your sneakers

Make sure the sneakers' surfaces are clean and free of dirt.

3. Prep your stencil

Prepare the stencil by spraying its back with spray adhesive. Allow the adhesive to dry 1 to 2 minutes, and then place the stencil on the sneaker where you would like to paint your design.

4. Color

Stained by Sharpie Fabric Markers are ideal and very easy to use on canvas or any type of cloth footwear. The narrow brush allows for use with even my most detailed stencils. Just color in the open areas of the stencil—simple!

Once you have filled in all the cutout areas, carefully lift the stencil to view your work. If the color is too light, reposition the stencil in the same place and apply more color.

5. Finish

Heat seal with a hair dryer for 2 minutes.

6. Clean up and kick it out

Wipe your stencil to remove any excess ink, and lay flat to dry. Now try on those kicks and skip down the street in style.

NEW YORK
PARIS
LONDON
HONG KONG
MILAN
BROOKLYN

Faux What?

Deface a Luxury Handbag

OVERVIEW

What could be more luxurious than ruining or defacing something of value? It's like cleaning the house in a Dior gown or pulling a Tallulah Bankhead and using money as toilet paper (yeah, I'm old!). Lady Gaga graffiti-tagged a $5,000 Hermès bag, so act like a rock star and follow along!

For this tutorial, I used a faux Louis Vuitton bag I found at a thrift store in Brooklyn. (Okay, I'm not *that* decadent.) LV has released tagged versions of its bags, but come on, let's do the fun part ourselves!

This tutorial shows you how to stencil on leather. Once you've done that, you might consider adding studs and other embellishments.

MATERIALS

- Leather material or apparel or accessory
- Rubber gloves
- Cotton ball or small rag
- Rubbing alcohol or acetone
- Sandpaper
- Water-based acrylics, specialty leather paint (such as Flashe brand) or spray paint (with mixed results)
- Paintbrush
- Stencil
- Paper towels
- Stencil brush, foam brush, or pouncer foam brush
- Hair dryer

INSTRUCTIONS

1. Prepare the leather

First, clean the leather area you will be painting with a slightly damp cloth and warm, soapy water.

2. Take off the shine

Some leather, especially if brand new, is waxy or shiny. This oil prevents paint from adhering to the surface and must be removed. Wearing rubber gloves, wipe the area with a cotton ball or small rag dipped in rubbing alcohol to remove this wax and oil. Acetone is another option. Then lightly sand the area with sandpaper. This makes the leather more porous so the paint will adhere and gives the leather a slightly distressed look.

3. Paint a prep layer

Before stenciling your design on the leather, you will need to paint the area with a prep layer. Mix one part water with one part paint, and brush the leather's surface using a paintbrush. You can match the color of this layer to the leather's color if you'd like. Apply two coats and let dry just until damp.

4. Stencil time

Lay your leather surface area flat and place the stencil where you want your design to appear. Using water-based acrylics or specialty leather paint, load a very small amount of paint onto your stencil brush, and dab most off on a paper towel. Now, in an up-and-down motion, paint in the open areas of the stencil.

A quick and dirty alternative is to use spray paint. I sprayed a heavy layer of pink paint on this LV bag until it ran. WE LOVE THE DRIPS! Once that layer dried, I placed the stencil over the pink area and taped it in place. I chose to mask the outer areas and control the overspray. I sprayed a darker color into the stencil. Take that, Luxury!

When you're finished, lift the stencil to reveal the design. Wipe your stencil clean of paint. Once the design dries, carefully flex the leather. Applying additional layers beyond the second one is up to you. Let each layer dry in between applications.

5. Seal it

Now, to make sure it all stays on, heat seal the design with a hair dryer, 1 to 2 minutes on all painted areas.

6. Take it further

Add pyramid spikes, safety pins, paint splashes, or your own tag.

7. Reveal

Once your paint is dry, you're ready to hit the streets in style. Now, swing that bag like you mean it.

In the Hood

Appliqué a Hoodie

OVERVIEW

A hoodie makes a statement no matter who is wearing it: hip-hop-preneur, celebrity in hiding, or icy fashion model. There's no wrong way to rock the hood. In this how-to, we show you a cool new way to max out your favorite sweatshirt for a layered designer look: appliqué.

Derived from the French word for "applied," appliqué is the technique of applying fabric or ornamentation to a garment. With stencils and felt, there's really no limit to the ways you can ornament your hoodie. But we've got a few ideas to get you started.

MATERIALS

- Stencil
- Wool felt in at least two colors
- Hooded sweatshirt
- Two-sided iron-on interfacing or fusible web (available at fabric stores)
- Iron
- Spray adhesive or masking tape
- Pencil or fabric chalk
- Scissors
- Fabric glue
- Thread or embroidery floss in colors to match the felt
- Sewing needle
- Straight pins

Note: Wool felt (available at fabric stores and a little more expensive) is preferred to acrylic craft felt (available at craft stores and less expensive) for this tutorial. Wool felt is higher quality and longer lasting than acrylic, and recommended for garments.

INSTRUCTIONS

1. Plan your design

For this appliqué project, you will be cutting out shapes from felt and layering them to create the look of the stenciled design. Begin by choosing a stencil with large open areas and a strong graphic element, like the crown stencil. The more tiny details in the stencil, the more tiny pieces you will have to cut out and sew. You may want to practice with paper before graduating to fabric.

Next, decide which color felt will be the base color and which color, or colors, you will use for the details, depending on the color of your sweatshirt and where you want to position it. Maybe you'd like your design on the back or the lapel. Or maybe you want to place it on the hood so people can see the design as you flip your hood and walk away. Think of the base color as your silhouette or background and the detail colors as your paint. The base color will be a solid shape, while the detail color will be the shapes from the open area of the stencil. The detail shapes will fit on the base like the pieces of a puzzle. You may also choose to not have a background layer and just apply the stencil cut out shapes to your sweatshirt.

2. Fusing

Once you've decided on a stencil and fabric, follow the directions of the interfacing or fusible web and iron one side of the fusing to your base felt. Leave the paper backing in place until you're ready to apply your appliqué to your hoodie.

3. Trace and trim

Spray the stencil with adhesive, wait 30 seconds, and position it on the detail fabric. Trace the open areas with a pencil or fabric chalk and peel up the stencil. With sharp scissors, cut out the pieces you traced. Spray the stencil with adhesive again, and this time, position the stencil on the felt side of your base fabric. Again, trace the open areas of the stencil with a pencil or tailor's chalk, and then remove the stencil.

Place a small dot of fabric glue on the back, or "wrong," side of each detail piece and match it to its traced area on the base fabric. Once all the detail pieces are in place, trim around the outside edge of the design, leaving a 1/8-in/3-mm border.

4. Stitching time

Allow the fabric glue to dry. Then hand-stitch the detail pieces in place on the base fabric. Here's where you can get creative. Use coordinating or contrasting thread or embroidery floss, depending on the look you want.

5. Keep calm and iron on

Heat the iron to the temperature appropriate for the fabric of your garment. Mark with pins where you'd like your appliqué to go, and lay your hoodie flat on the ironing board.

Peel off the paper backing, position the appliqué, and press it into place with the hot iron. If your appliqué is very thick, you may need to press it from the underside of the fabric.

Now, stitch along the outer edge of the base fabric, making sure the appliqué is attached securely to your garment. This step will ensure that your appliqué stands up to repeat washing.

6. Step out in style

Throw on your sweatshirt, pull up your hood, and hit the streets!

Glitter Train

Give Sparkle Motion to a Suit Jacket

OVERVIEW

When you hear the name Martha Stewart, you may think Queen of Craft, home stylist extraordinaire, perfectionist, domestic doyenne. . . . But what about fashionista? Well, did you know Martha Stewart started out as a fashion model? A drop-dead-gorgeous one, in fact.

The Queen of Craft often features our stencils in her projects, so we're going to spotlight one of our favorites and take it up a notch: children's glittery stenciled tees with Martha's premium glitter. Since metallics and shine are always in style, don't think glitter is just for kids—in this project, we show you how it works for an evening suit jacket!

MATERIALS

- ○ Cardboard, shipping box, or shirt box
- ○ Suit jacket
- ○ Stencil
- ○ Masking tape
- ○ Stencil brush, foam brush, or pouncer foam brush
- ○ Washable fabric glue
- ○ Glitter or glass beads from Martha Stewart Crafts
- ○ Paper plate or tray

Note: For this project, we used a tuxedo jacket we found in a thrift store, but any type of blazer, suit coat, or sport coat will work beautifully.

INSTRUCTIONS

1. Prep and position

Place a piece of cardboard, a shipping box, or a shirt box inside your suit jacket to protect the other layers of the jacket. If your jacket has a detached lining (check the bottom hem for an opening), insert the cardboard between the lining and the body fabric. Now, place the jacket on a flat, clean work surface. Position your stencil where you'd like your design to be, and tape in place with masking tape.

2. Apply glue and glitter

Using your stencil brush or foam pouncer, apply fabric glue in the open areas of the stencil. Sprinkle glitter or glass beads over the glue and shake off the excess onto a paper plate or tray. Feel free to combine colors! You can use the leftover glitter for other projects or more glitter apparel!

3. Peel and seal

Peel up the stencil from the jacket and let the glue dry completely before wearing. Wipe excess glue from the stencil while the glue is still wet.

4. Strut

Put that sparkle in motion!

Bedazzle Me

Bejewel a Sweater

Guest Artist: Leslie Hall

OVERVIEW

Fashion has a tongue-in-cheek, campy, and ironic flip side to its glamorous, sophisticated image. Styles get reinvented, turned upside down, and called retro. Featured guest Leslie Hall has taken former fashion pariahs—shiny spandex and gem sweaters—and made them de rigueur. Leslie is a musical amazement, as well as a fashion revolutionary, who has blessed the world with addictive dance beats, including a song praising her beloved gem sweater.

Gem sweaters conjure up painful and gorgeous images of glam grandmas rockin' dazzling duds, and Leslie wears hers with style. She even curates the Gem Sweater Museum. We are honored to learn how to make a sparkly gem sweater from the master.

MATERIALS

- Colorful sweater or sweatshirt
- Stencil, preferably a bold design
- Cardboard, shipping box, or shirt box
- Fabric chalk
- Fabric glue or puff paint
- Gems, studs, or sequins

Note: Blast Leslie Hall's dance track "Gem Sweater" to get you in the mood!

INSTRUCTIONS

1. Choose your palette

Select a colorful, fun sweater or sweatshirt to embellish. Next, choose a stencil design to use as a guide for your gems. A detailed stencil design might not appear clearly when you use gems, so go with a pattern or bolder image. Place the stencil where you want the design to appear.

2. Prep your surface

Stretch your sweater over a piece of rectangular cardboard, a shipping box, or a shirt box to prevent glue from seeping through to the back of the garment. This will also provide a flat working surface. To avoid warping your design, don't stretch the sweater too much. Using fabric chalk, draw the outline of the stencil's open areas onto your sweater. These shapes will hold the coveted gems!

3. Bedazzle!

With fabric glue or puff paint, adhere the gems inside the shapes you drew until all the shapes are filled in completely. Let dry for 24 hours.

4. Strut your stuff

Wear your dazzling gem sweater—it goes with just about everything—and dance!

Star Spangled Bangles

Decorate Bracelets for a Night on the Town

OVERVIEW

A wristful of bracelets is hot. And customizing your bangles will ensure that they have the maximum effect. In this fun and easy tutorial, we'll show you how to create star-spangled bangles that will be the envy of even the flashiest diva.

MATERIALS

- Plain, paintable bangles with a wide surface area
- Fine-grain sandpaper (if recycling thrift-store bangles)
- Damp coth and dry towel
- Stained by Sharpie Fabric Markers, enamel paint, or spray paint
- Small stencils
- Clothespins or binder clips
- Masking tape
- Spray adhesive
- Stencil brush (if using paint)
- Glitter*
- Clear polyurethane sealant spray*

*optional

Note: You can find wood or plastic bangles at thrift stores and craft stores, or online at shops like www.diybangles.com

INSTRUCTIONS

1. Prep your surface

Lightly scuff the surface of the bangles with sandpaper to remove any existing paint or if your bangle has a slick surface. Wipe away any debris with a damp cloth and dry with a towel. (You can skip the sanding step if you're working with a virgin bangle.) Now, paint a base color on your bangle, if you prefer, and allow it to dry.

2. Position your stencil

Wrapping a stencil around a curvy bangle isn't easy. Take your time and be patient; the results will be worth it. Position your stencil on a small section of the bangle. Secure the stencil in place with clothespins or binder clips, depending on the thickness of your bangle. A little masking tape may aid in securing your stencil as well. For a really secure fit, spray the back of the stencil with adhesive spray, allow to dry until tacky to the touch, then adhere to the bangle.

3. Paint and sparkle

With your markers or stencil brush, carefully fill in the open areas of the stencil design. Sprinkle in a little glitter for extra shine, if you'd like. Repeat Steps 2 and 3 until the bangle is decorated to your heart's desire.

4. Get set

If you used enamel paint, it will need at least 4 hours to dry; markers will be dry immediately. Optional: Spray a layer of clear polyurethane sealant for a glossy polished look. Wait the proper amount of time before wearing your bangles, or you'll have smudging and sadness. And no one likes a sad disco queen.

5. Hit the disco

When they're good to go, stack those spangly bangles up your arm and hit the street. The world is your dance floor!

33

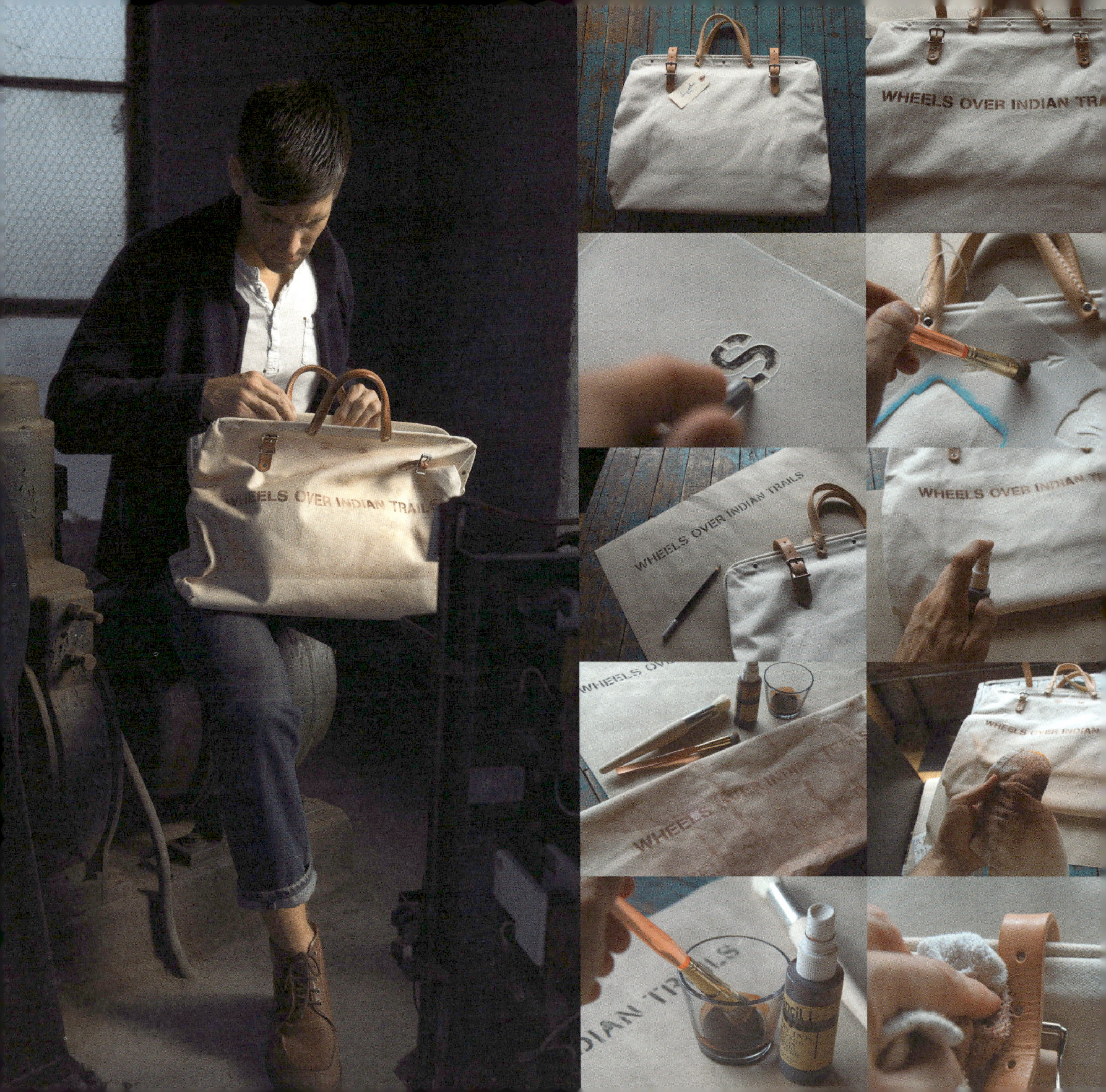

WHEELS OVER INDIAN TRAILS
WHEELS OVER INDIAN TRAILS
WHEELS OVER INDIAN TRAILS
WHEELS OVER INDIAN TRAILS
WHEELS OVER INDIAN TRAILS
WHEELS OVER INDIAN
INDIAN TRAILS

So Distressed

Refashion a Men's Canvas Work Bag

Guest Artist: Lucy Thompson of Sidney & Sons

OVERVIEW

A rugged canvas bag is a stylish and practical accessory for any guy. It's even cooler if it's been in the family for a hundred years. But what if Grandpa or Uncle Jed didn't leave you his well-worn rucksack? Then Sidney & Sons can save your fashion reputation.

Sidney & Sons create bags that are utilitarian in essence and modern in design. All of the pieces are handmade in New York City. Their bags are the perfect blank canvas for stenciling, with their clean lines and seemingly effortless design.

Using her exceptional taste, Lucy Thompson of Sidney & Sons has created this custom-stenciled-bag tutorial. Best of all, this how-to is fast and simple, since canvas is the easiest thing to paint. It takes shabby chic to its natural, masculine conclusion.

And as for the bag pictured, I chose to write "Wheels Over Indian Trails," the words of innovative artist John Fekner who has created hundreds of outdoor works consisting of stenciled words and spray paint. Fekner's stencil Wheels Over Indian Trails greeted motorists and international travelers arriving in New York City at the Pulaski Bridge Queens Midtown Tunnel from 1979 to 1990. The message remained untouched for eleven years, until Earth Day 1990, when Mr. Fekner, feeling the piece had run its course, painted over it. Idol!

Note: Sidney & Sons' wares are available at www.etsy.com/shop/sidneyandsons.

MATERIALS

- ○ **Canvas bag**
- ○ **Cardboard**
- ○ **Stencil**
- ○ **Spray adhesive, masking** or **painter's tape**
- ○ **Stencil brushes, foam brushes,** or **pouncer foam brushes**
- ○ **Fabric paint** or **Stencil1 Sprayers**
- ○ **Thick paper, cardboard,** or **poster board to control overspray** (if spray-painting)
- ○ **Safety goggles** (if spray-painting)
- ○ **Iron** or **hair dryer**

INSTRUCTIONS

1. Get bag and stencil ready

Lay your canvas bag on a flat work surface and slip a piece of cardboard into the bag to provide a flat surface to stencil. This will also prevent paint seepage to the inside of the bag. Place your stencil where you want the design to appear on the bag, and adhere with spray adhesive. You may also secure it in place with masking or painter's tape. If you use spray adhesive, apply a light layer to the back of the stencil. Allow the adhesive to dry until the surface becomes tacky, and then position your stencil.

2. Paint!

Using a stencil brush and fabric paint, fill in the open areas of the stencil, using a small amount of paint at a time. Apply multiple layers of paint to intensify the color, rather than applying thick coats. Alternatively, you can use Stencil1 Sprayers to fill in your design. If using the spray method, use some thick paper to mask out the outer areas of the stencil to control overspray. Spray into the open areas 6 to 8 in/15 to 20 cm from the surface until cutout areas are filled. Remember to wear your goggles. Carefully lift your stencil to prevent paint from dripping.

3. Finish

Allow the paint to dry completely. Then, before using, heat press the design by turning the bag inside out and ironing the inside of the painted area. Set your iron on high heat and press for 1 to 2 minutes. You can also blow-dry the inside of the bag with a hair dryer for 1 to 2 minutes.

4. Carry on

Show this bag off on your commute, the design side strategically facing all envious eyes!

36

Silky Touch

Create a Pattern on a Silk Scarf

OVERVIEW

The printed silk scarf is a signature accessory of many leading design houses, like Hermès, Louis Vuitton, and Versace (pronounced Ver-sayse!). From repeating geometric and floral patterns to the house logo, each brand has its own unique approach to this essential fashion accessory. In this tutorial, we'll show you how to paint a repeat pattern on silk to get that high-style look for a down-market price.

MATERIALS

- Iron
- Solid-colored silk scarf
- Cardboard or craft paper
- Stencil
- Spray adhesive
- Masking tape
- Scrap paper
- Stencil1 Sprayers or fabric paint for silk
- Stencil brushes (if using fabric paint)
- Paper towels

INSTRUCTIONS

1. Prep your material

Iron the silk scarf on a very low heat to provide a nice, flat surface for stenciling. Because the fabric is thin, the ink or paint may seep through onto your work surface. Place a piece of cardboard or craft paper under the scarf to protect the surface before you begin painting. Lay the scarf out flat.

2. Plan your design

Think about what you want your pattern to be. Maybe you want to use an image that repeats in rows, or maybe you want to alternate between two or three designs. It's up to you. I like to sketch my design idea on paper first, or even stencil it on a piece of cardboard before I move on to the real deal. A practice run is never a bad idea.

3. Set the stencil

Now, place your first stencil where you'd like the design to start. Silk is very delicate, so go light if using spray adhesive on the back of the stencil. (As an alternative, you can weigh down the stencil with stacks of quarters or other small items of similar weight.) To control overspray, mask the outer edges of the stencil by taping scrap paper to the stencil and covering the remaining fabric. Spray has a way of creeping under the stencil, so the tape is important.

4. Paint

Shake the Stencil1 Sprayer; then, holding the bottle 6 to 8 in/15 to 20 cm from the stencil, begin to spray the open areas of the stencil with a sweeping motion. Go lightly on the paint, as the silk is absorbent—too much will cause the design to bleed and will result in blurry edges. If brush painting, use very little paint on your brush, a little goes a long way. Brush paint in the open areas of the stencil until filled.

5. Rinse and repeat

Carefully lift the stencil without bending or "peeling," so as to prevent the excess ink remaining on the stencil from dripping. Blot the excess ink with a paper towel; clean and dry the stencil.

Once the ink on the scarf is dry, continue by positioning the stencil in the next place in your pattern. Repeat the painting process until your pattern is to your liking. Use as many stencils as you desire. It's your design house!

6. Set it (but don't forget it)

Let the ink dry completely. Iron again on a low heat to seal the design. Tie your scarf on a designer bag or around your neck like a '50s flight attendant, or wrap it on your head like Little Edie Beale. However you wear it, wear it with style.

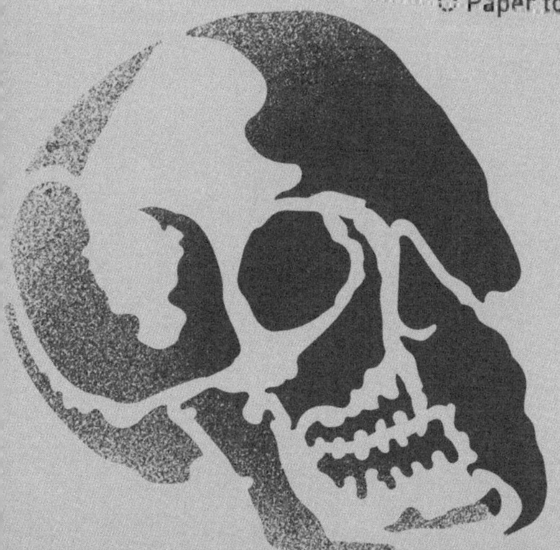

Totes!

Customize a Grocery Tote

OVERVIEW

Plastic grocery bags simply are not fashion! What *is* fashion: carrying your groceries home in your own tote bag. My shopping tip for you and for this tutorial is to run to MUJI and buy their cloth tote bags—you can get them for pocket change!

MATERIALS

- Cloth tote bag
- Cardboard
- Stencil
- Spray adhesive or painter's tape
- Stencil brushes, foam brushes, or pouncer foam brushes
- Fabric paint or Stencil1 Sprayers
- Thick paper, cardboard, or poster board to control overspray (if spray-painting)
- Safety goggles (if spray-painting)
- Iron or hair dryer

INSTRUCTIONS

1. Get bag and stencil ready

Lay your tote bag on a flat work surface and slip a piece of cardboard into the bag to provide a flat surface to stencil. This will also prevent paint seepage to the back of the bag. Place your stencil where you want the design to appear on the bag, and adhere with spray adhesive. You may also secure it in place with masking or painter's tape.

2. Paint!

Using a stencil brush and fabric paint, fill in the open areas of the stencil, using a small amount of paint at a time. Apply multiple layers of paint to intensify the color, rather than applying thick coats. Alternatively, you can use Stencil1 Sprayers to fill in your design. If using the spray method, use some scrap paper to mask out the outer areas of the stencil to control overspray. Spray into the open areas 6 to 8 in/15 to 20 cm from the surface until cutout areas are filled. Don't forget to wear your goggles. Carefully lift your stencil to prevent paint from dripping.

3. Finish

Allow the paint to dry completely. Then, before using, heat press the design by turning the bag inside out and ironing the inside of the painted area. Set your iron on high heat and press for 1 to 2 minutes. You can also blow-dry the inside of the bag with a hair dryer for 1 to 2 minutes.

4. Shop

Be a green shopper with your new, fashionable tote!

All Puffed Up

Quilt Your Favorite Winter Coat

OVERVIEW

When most people think of quilting, they envision grandmothers sitting in a circle, stitching big quilts with country motifs of stars and log cabins. But that's not all it's about. The art of quilting is also about modern-day fashion. Think puffy ski jackets and snowboarders ripping through the powder in their neon finery, or chic New Yorkers knocking off the chill with their nipped-and-tucked winterwear. Quilting, which is simply sewing together layers of fabric, allows you to introduce texture, dimension, and design to your garments.

Starting with an insulated jacket and a stencil, you can give your outerwear a quilted look with this tutorial. Basically, you are drawing with your sewing machine. Let's get started!

MATERIALS

- Insulated jacket
- Masking tape
- Stencil
- Tailor's chalk or pencil
- Straight pins
- Sewing machine
- Thread
- Scissors

INSTRUCTIONS

1. Pick your jacket
Make sure you choose a coat that's not too puffy, so it will fit your sewing machine. We don't all have a commercial design studio!

2. Choose your position
Tape your stencil on the jacket where you'd like the design to appear, and trace the open areas with tailor's chalk or a pencil.

3. Pin it
Since you're working with layers, it's best to pin the layers together so they don't bunch up and get weird while you're sewing. Quilters call this step "basting." Starting at the center of your design and working your way out to the edge, place a straight pin every 2 in/5 cm along the lines you've drawn. Smooth out any wrinkles.

4. Quilt
Thread your sewing machine with the color thread you'd like to use on your design. Stitch along the traced lines, pulling out the pins as you go. For a subtle look, match the thread color to the color of your jacket. You're quilting.

5. Finish
When you come to the end of the design, run back and forth over the last couple of stitches to secure them, and cut your thread with the scissors. You're all done. Now, put on your one-of-a-kind winter creation, and you'll be the hit of the après-ski scene.

Tie One On

Embellish a Men's Tie

OVERVIEW

Ties are an essential men's accessory, and some guys collect them the way women collect shoes. What could be better than to have a tie that no one else has? So make your own design, and when asked, "Who makes that tie?" you can say, "An amazing designer—me!"

MATERIALS

- ⟡ **Newspaper** or **butcher paper**
- ⟡ **Cotton** or **wool tie**
- ⟡ **Stencil**
- ⟡ **Spray Adhesive** or **masking tape**
- ⟡ **Stencil1 Sprayers**
- ⟡ **Scrap paper**
- ⟡ **Iron**

INSTRUCTIONS

1. Prep your space

Spread newspaper or butcher paper on a table to create a working area.

2. Choose your style

A cotton or wool tie gives the best results. You can stencil over a solid color, or it might be fun to stencil over a pattern, such as stripes or polka dots. Let your creativity lead the way. Lay the tie flat on your work surface.

3. Place the stencil

Choose a small stencil design that fits on the tie, or a larger design that extends past the tie's edges for a bold or abstract look. Pick your stencil and spray a light mist of adhesive on the back. Let the adhesive dry 30 to 60 seconds, and then place the stencil on the tie where you would like the design to appear. If you prefer, you can position the stencil with masking tape.

4. Start painting

Stencil1 Sprayers are ideal for this project, since they apply pigment lightly and evenly. The metallic sprays might add an element of fun to your project, but it's up to you, designer. (You could also use a stencil brush and fabric paint as an alternative to spray pigments, but we opted for the sprayed look.)

Once you've chosen your color(s), cover any areas outside the stencil with scrap paper to avoid overspray, and tape down the edges with masking tape. Spray paints find their way under the paper if you do not tape it well.

Holding the sprayer 6 to 8 in/ 15 to 20 cm away at a 45-degree angle, spray in a sweeping motion. Repeat until the design area is filled with paint and the color isthe intensity you desire.

5. Clean up

Lift the stencil, taking care to keep it horizontal to your work to avoid spilling the excess ink off the stencil and onto your beautiful project. Wipe the stencil off with a slightly damp cloth, and dry flat.

6. Heat treat, meet, and greet

Once the ink is dry, heat seal it by pressing it with an iron on medium heat for 1 to 2 minutes. Then tie one on, you dapper thing!

All for the Money

Customize a Leather Wallet

Guest Artist: Stella Zotis

OVERVIEW

You may know Stella Zotis as the rockin' "leatha" designer from *Project Runway*, but what that show might not have revealed about Stella is that she is an incredibly talented artisan. I recently stopped by Stella's red-walled studio to learn some leather tricks and was blown away by the art, banners, bags, and dresses she has created. So much of it resonated with me, since many of her pieces incorporate cutout leather images applied to garments. But let me be clear: Stella does not (normally) use stencils. She cuts and sews all her designs freehand!

I went expecting a lesson in leather appliqué, and Stella graciously showed me how to make an entire wallet from scratch. Now, we're sharing it with you. For more inspiration, you can check out Stella's entire collection at www.stellazotis.com.

MATERIALS

- American cowhide leather in three colors
- Wallet template, found online at www.chronicle books.com/stencilstyle
- Scissors
- Stencil
- Fabric marker or tailor's chalk
- Fabric glue or regular school glue
- Sewing machine that can handle leather, ideally with a walking foot
- Thread
- Grommet kit and pyramid studs*

*optional

Note: Leather has two sides: a shiny, tanned side and a "fuzzy," suede side. In this tutorial, the terms "right side," "face up," and "out" all refer to the tanned side of the leather. Placing the tanned side out is more practical for an item like a wallet, since it's more resistant to stains, water, and wear.

Note: Stella's favorite online resource for American cowhide is www.tandy leatherfactory.com.

INSTRUCTIONS

1. Choose the leather

Stella prefers to work with American cowhide. For this project, we used less than a 2-ft/0.3-m square of black leather for our wallet body and two small pieces of red and white leather for our stencil design—about 4 by 4 in/10 by 10 cm of each color.

2. Cutting by numbers

Measure and cut your leather pieces according to the template. You will need the following cuts of leather: two 4-by-8-in/10-by-20-cm black pieces (outer and inner folds); one 4-by-3-in/10-by-7.5-cm black piece (inner pocket); one 3-by-2½-in/7-by-6-cm black piece (inner cardholder large); one 2½-by-2½-in/6-by-6-cm black piece (inner cardholder small); one 4-by-4-in/10-by-10-cm red piece (star design); one 4-by-4-in/10-by-10-cm white piece (circle design). Alternately, you can make a wallet of your own custom dimensions.

3. Time to stencil

Lay the leather you're using for your stencil design facedown on a flat surface (in our case, the red leather). Place the stencil (we're using the star stencil) on top of the leather and trace the stencil design with a fabric marker or tailor's chalk. Cut out the design.

Referring to the template, trace and cut out the circle. Place the cutout on the suede side of your contrasting leather color (white for us), and trace the circle. Cut out

[CONT.]

45

your perfect white circle, and you have the components for a two-layered design!

4. Glue it

Even though you are going to sew them, it's best to glue the cutouts together so the pieces do not shift while sewing, or separate and bubble later. Spread a thin layer of fabric glue evenly on the back of the star. Place the star in the center of the circle on the right side, and press out the wrinkles with your fingers. Allow to dry at least 1 hour.

5. Assemble the outer fold

Place your two-layer design under the sewing machine to attach the star to the circle. Starting at a point, sew a straight line, about eight stitches long, along the edge of the design, then turn the design and sew along the next straight line of the star. Turning at each point, continue until you make it all the way around.

Once the star is sewn to the circle, it's time to attach the entire design to the wallet "face." Take one 4-by-8-in/10-by-20-cm piece of leather and fold it in half, suede-side in, so you can imagine the wallet as it will look when it's completed. Glue the design to the face of your wallet where you'd like the design to appear. Let the glue dry as before, then hit the sewing machine again to attach the circle to the wallet face. You've completed the outer fold of your wallet!

6. Assemble the inner fold

Our wallet has two cardholders and one side pocket on the inside fold (see template for reference). Lay the second 4-by-8-in/10-by-20-cm cut of leather faceup on your work surface, and position the 4-by-3-in/10-by-7.5-cm inner pocket, also faceup, flush right on the base piece. Sew together on three sides (top, right, and bottom) to attach the pocket to the base, leaving the left side open, creating the pocket.

On the left side of the base piece, position the 3-by-2½-in/7-by-6-cm (large) cardholder piece where you'd like it to be, and sew the pieces together on three sides (left, bottom, and right), leaving the top open for cards. Next, place the 2½-by-2½-in/6-by-6-cm (small) cardholder piece on top of the large one, flush with the bottom edge, and sew the pieces together on three sides (left, bottom, and right), leaving the top open for more cards. You have completed the inner fold of the wallet.

7. Assemble the wallet

Place the outer- and inner-fold pieces together, suede to suede, and sew three sides together (left, bottom, and right), leaving the top open for your cash. Fold the wallet in half, and you're done!

To take your wallet to another level, Stella suggests adding a grommet so you can attach a chain. Grommet kits are available online and at most hardware or craft stores. Here's how to add a grommet: You'll need a work surface that can withstand hammering. Place the leather on a scrap piece of wood and, using the hole cutter and a hammer, punch a hole in the leather where you'd like the chain to connect. Insert the two pieces of the grommet into the hole you created. The piece with the "tube" goes through the right side of the leather; the ring goes on the wrong side, on top of the tube. Place the anvil (the thick metal disk) under the tube side of the grommet, and the mandrel (the long metal cone) in the tube protrusion. With a hammer or rubber mallet, give the mandrel a few good whacks (five is the recommended number), and voilà—you've got a grommet that's perfect for a wallet chain.

8. Flash your cash

Now you have a custom money holder worthy of your creative spirit. Thank you, Stella!

These Boots Were Made for Walkin'

Personalize Leather or Suede Boots

OVERVIEW

Years ago, a customer of mine sent me a picture of UGGs she had stenciled with my hummingbird design. They were so cool—like the fashionista version of decorating your Vans in high school. In that spirit, this tutorial will show you how to stencil suede or leather combat boots. It's similar to the process for leather accessories and yields some really fun results.

MATERIALS

- Leather or suede boots
- Rubber gloves (if using leather)
- Cotton ball or small rag (if using leather)
- Rubbing alcohol or acetone (if using leather)
- Fine-grain sandpaper (if using leather)
- Stiff wire brush (if using suede)
- Water-based acrylics or specialty leather paint (such as Flashe brand)*
- Paintbrush
- Stencil
- Spray adhesive or masking tape
- Stencil brush, foam brush, or pouncer foam brush
- Paper towels
- Fabric glue

*Alternatively, you can use spray paint.

INSTRUCTIONS

For Leather (see below for suede)

1a. Clean

First, clean the leather surface area you will be painting with a slightly damp cloth and warm, soapy water.

2a. Take off the shine

Some leather, especially if brand new, is waxy or shiny. This oil prevents paint from adhering to the surface and must be removed. Wearing rubber gloves, wipe the areas with a cotton ball or small rag dipped in rubbing alcohol to remove this wax and oil. Acetone is another option. Then lightly sand the area with sandpaper. This makes the leather more porous so the paint will adhere and gives the leather a slightly distressed look.

For Suede

1b. Clean

Using a stiff wire brush, brush suede, taking all strokes in the same direction to remove dirt and debris.

2b. Suede is matte, not shiny, and doesn't much like water

Go straight to Step 4!

3. Paint a prep layer

Before stenciling your design on leather, you will need to paint a prep layer. Mix one part water with one part paint, and brush the surface using a paintbrush. You can match the color of this layer to the leather's color if you'd like. Apply two coats and let dry just until damp.

4. Stenciling time

Lay the paintable surface area of the boot as flat as possible. Pick your stencil and spray a light mist of adhesive on the back. Let the adhesive dry 30 to 60 seconds, and then place the stencil on the boot where you would like the design to appear. If you prefer, you can position the stencil with masking tape. Using water-based acrylics or specialty leather paint, load a very small amount of paint onto your stencil brush, and dab some off on a paper towel. Now, in an up-and-down motion, paint in the open areas of the stencil. (Alternatively, you can use spray paint, but it may not have lasting results.) Lift your stencil, and wipe clean of paint. Realign it in the same place as last time and apply another layer. Applying additional layers beyond the second one is up to you. Let it dry. Once the design dries, carefully flex the leather or suede.

5. Walk for me

Now, stomp that @&¢#$. Runway!

A Stitch in Time

Knit with Intarsia

Guest Artist: Leigh Angel

OVERVIEW

Knitting, sewing, stenciling, and . . . editing? My friend Leigh Angel is one of the many multifaceted jewels I am fortunate to work with. Not only does she help me with my writing, but she can take on the tallest of crafts. Her main creative weapons are knitting needles and yarn, so when I asked her to show us how to convert a stencil into an intarsia knitting pattern, she rocked out these fingerless gloves.

Leigh taught herself to knit and crochet in adulthood, though creating has been a lifelong obsession. In the summer of 2011, she took her needle-arts skills to Rwanda, teaching crochet to the girls at the Ubushobozi Project, and has plans to go back in 2012 to teach knitting. You can keep up with her adventures in handmade at Leighangel.wordpress.com. Take it away, Leigh.

Intarsia is a colorwork method that incorporates images into knitted fabric. By transferring an image to a chart, you can knit the design into a garment. Intarsia can be used with scarves, gloves, mittens, hats, sweaters . . . the list is endless.

The difference between intarsia and its color-work cousin, Fair Isle, is how the yarn is handled while knitting. Instead of carrying the yarn behind the design, which creates bulk and thumb-catching strings, the strands of yarn are twisted together whenever colors are changed, leaving your fabric stretchy and light. You'll catch on as we go, so let's get started.

Note: For additional references on intarsia technique, check out www.planetpurl.com and watch the Intro to Intarsia Knitting and Wind a Butterfly videos. For gauge-specific knitting graph paper, visit www.knitonthenet.com/designchart.

MATERIALS

○ **Cherry Pop Fingerless Glove pattern with intarsia chart** (www.chroniclebooks.com/stencilstyle)
○ **DK yarn** (one 50-g ball of main color and two contrasting colors, at least 4 yd/3.5 m each)
○ **U.S. size 5 (3.75 mm) knitting needles**, or **size to obtain gauge**
○ **Knitting graph paper**
○ **Stencil**
○ **Pencil**

INSTRUCTIONS

1. Choose your tools

Intarsia works with almost any kind of knitting project, whatever your skill level, though it plays most nicely when knitted flat in stockinette stitch (knit a row, purl a row, repeat). The technique kicks up beginner projects to advanced-beginner status. Choose a project you feel comfortable with, and the appropriate yarn and needles. I created these easy fingerless gloves for the beginning knitter, and chose soft, durable, DK-weight merino wool in three colors, along with size 5 (3.75 mm) knitting needles.

2. Chart your design

Standard graph paper is made of little squares. Knitting stitches are wider than they are tall, so knitting graph paper is made of little rectangles. To chart your own designs for intarsia, you'll need to use knitting graph paper; otherwise, your designs could come out warped. Fear not! We've provided a sheet of knitting graph paper, along with the cherries chart, so you can get started right away.

Gauge is important for making knitted garments that fit, as well as for charting designs so they fit within your project. For example, the gauge for the gloves is 20 stitches and 28 rows in a 4-in/10-cm square, and our pattern calls for us to cast on 40 stitches. That means the fabric is going to be 8 in/20 cm across. The design should appear on only one-half of the glove, so the image should be fewer than 20 stitches across.

When you chart the design, it should take up fewer than twenty squares on the graph paper. The same accommodations should be made for the height of the design. The bulkier the yarn, the fewer the stitches your design can handle. The finer the yarn, the more detailed your design can be.

Place the stencil you'd like to chart over the graph paper and trace the outline. Then pencil in the squares inside the outline with Xs. There are no half-stitches in knitting, so curved lines will be sharper than in reality—think pixelated 8-bit video game graphics. If a line cuts a square in half, use your best judgment—and a pencil with an eraser—when deciding where to put those questionable Xs. Draw an outline around the image to see if it's the right shape, then make adjustments if necessary.

[CONT.]

3. Decode the chart

Look at the cherries chart. Each box on the chart represents a stitch. Each row of boxes represents a row of knitting. The chart is read from bottom to top, and alternating right to left and left to right. Unless otherwise noted, odd-numbered (knit) rows are read from right to left, and even-numbered (purl) rows are read from left to right.

Next, determine where the color changes are. The cherries chart has three colors: the main, or background, color (MC), the cherry color (CC), and the stem color (SC). The first stitch in the first row of each cherry represents a color change, as does the first stitch of each stem. That equals four color changes so far.

What might be less obvious are the MC color changes. Every time the main color is dropped for a contrasting color, a new strand of the MC will be started on the other side. In the case of the cherries, there will be three working sections of MC: one at the beginning (MC1), one after the left-hand cherry (MC2), and one between the two cherries once the right-hand cherry begins (MC3).

4. Get twisted

The key to intarsia is in the twist. To make a color change, the strands of yarn are "twisted" together to prevent holes in the work and keep the yarn where you need it. But twisting can be a bit confusing. Let me explain.

Reading right to left, the first row of the cherries chart says to knit 9 stitches in the main color, 2 stitches in the cherry color, and 2 stitches in the main color again. Here's what you do: knit those 9 MC1 stitches. Then knit the next 2 stitches with the CC yarn and give the strands a little tug to tighten up. For added security, you can make a half-knot with the tail end of the new yarn and the old yarn when joining, or you can leave the tail loose and close the hole when weaving in ends. Knit the remaining 2 chart stitches with MC2, tugging up to tighten, and tie to the CC yarn if you desire.

Twisting happens properly on the second row of the chart. Reading left to right, row two says to purl 1 stitch of MC2, then 4 stitches of CC, then 8 stitches of MC1. After purling 1 MC2, lay the MC2 yarn over the CC strand, then bring the CC strand up and purl for the 4 stitches as directed. Then lay the CC strand over the MC1 strand, bring up the MC1 strand and continue purling to the end of the row.

Let me sum up: Twisting is laying the old yarn over the new yarn before stitching. Give the stitches a little tug to tighten up each time you change yarn. It's going to get crazy. Embrace the chaos.

5. Prepare to knit

Butterflies are small bits of yarn wound up for knitting up the colorwork so you don't have big balls of yarn hanging down from your needle. To make a butterfly, simply unwind a yard/meter or so of yarn from the ball and wrap in a figure 8 around your thumb and pinky finger. Then tie the tail around the center at the cross-point and pull off your fingers. You need a butterfly for each color-change section in your chart.

There will be several butterflies dangling from your needles at any given time, but don't panic! The tangles will all make sense as the picture begins to form. Any time it starts to feel too chaotic, stop and untangle the butterflies before you proceed.

The cherries chart requires five butterflies (see the online pattern for length): two cherry color, two stem color, and one main color, plus two half-balls of main color yarn. Cut the lengths of yarn and wrap them into butterflies before you begin. (Alternately, since the lengths are short, the yarn can be left to dangle, unwound.) Then divide the main color ball in half. You're ready to start knitting.

6. Knit and shout

Follow the accompanying knitting pattern (or your own), and before you know it, you'll have a sweet pair of gloves you'll be proud to sport in any weather.

CHERRY POP FINGERLESS GLOVES

MATERIALS

- ◊ **Debbie Bliss Rialto DK** (100% merino, superwash; 50 g: 25 yd/15 m)
- ◊ **1 ball main color** (divided into two balls and one 2-yd/1.75-m length)
- ◊ **6 yd/5 m cherries color** (two equal lengths)
- ◊ **4 yd/3.5 m stem color** (two equal lengths)
- ◊ **U.S. size 5 (3.75 mm) needle**, or **size necessary to obtain gauge**
- ◊ **Stitch markers**
- ◊ **Yarn needle**
- ◊ **Gauge: 20 stitches and 28 rows = 4 in/10 cm in stockinette stitch**

Finished measurements: approximately 7 in/18 cm long, 8 in/20 cm in circumference.

INSTRUCTIONS

CO 40 st in MC.

Cuff

Row 1: *K2, P2*, repeat to end of row.
Row 2: *K2, P2*, repeat to end of row.
Continue 2 x 2 rib for 2 in/5 cm.

Body

Next 2 rows:
K all stitches.
P all stitches.
Continue in stockinette stitch for 1 in/2.5 cm or until entire piece is about 3 in/7.5 cm.

Left-hand glove

Begin intarsia chart:
K4, PM, K first row of chart, PM, K23 to end of row.
P23 to first marker, P second row of chart to second marker, P4.
Continue in pattern to end of chart (22 rows).

Right-hand glove

Begin intarsia chart:
K23, PM, K first row of chart, PM, K4 to end of row.
P4 to first marker, P second row of chart to second marker, P23.
Continue in pattern to end of chart (22 rows).

Next row after chart

Continue in stockinette stitch for 6 rows; twist remaining strand from last intarsia row as first K row is worked.
Next 2 rows: *K2, P2*, repeat to end of row.
BO in pattern. Leave a long tail for seaming.

Weave in ends around intarsia pattern, tightening up any gaps around the design.

Seaming

With the wrong side facing, fold edges together lengthwise. Place a stitch marker or safety pin about 3 in/7.5 cm from the bottom cuff, and a second marker or pin about 3 in/7.5 cm from the top cuff. Sew the sides together with mattress stitch, leaving a thumbhole between the markers. Weave in the remaining ends. Block it and rock it.

Abbreviations

CO = cast on
MC = main color
K = knit
P = purl
PM = place marker
BO = bind off

Baby Never Felt Better

Needle Felt a Baby Sweater

OVERVIEW

Babies are the must-have accessory of the season, and to stay on trend, yours needs to be lookin' major. With a needle felted sweater, both you and your little bundle of chic will turn heads wherever you perambulate.

Needle felting is a fun and easy appliqué technique that sticks wool to wool without glue or sewing. Don't worry—all will become clear in the instructions. Once you have the know-how, you can embellish just about anything made of wool: sweaters, scarves, socks, hats, bags … the possibilities are endless!

Let's get started. Fashion waits for no baby.

MATERIALS

- **Wool baby sweater** or a **wool blend** (at least 50 percent)
- **Foam block** (a little bigger than the design area of the stencil and will fit inside your sweater)
- **Stencil**
- **Masking tape**
- **1 to 2 balls of wool roving** (raw wool that has yet to be spun into yarn) **in colors of your choice**
- **Size 38 felting needle**

Note: A wool sweater is important so that the fibers of the roving tangle with the fibers of the sweater, creating a lasting appliqué. Wool roving can be purchased at most craft and hobby stores or online in kits of multiple colors. Two 0.22-oz/6-g balls of roving (about the size of tennis balls) will be more than enough for this project.

INSTRUCTIONS

1. Prep and position

With the right side of the sweater fabric facing up, place the foam block inside the sweater or, if you are using a cardigan, under the side where you'd like the design to appear. Position your stencil and secure with masking tape.

2. Choose your weapons

Once you're satisfied with the stencil's placement, take a small pinch of roving and place it in one of the open areas of the stencil. With the felting needle, lightly stab the roving into the sweater. Essentially, you are pushing the loose fibers into the sweater and tangling them together. Doing this repeatedly creates a design.

The amount of roving you use determines how thick the appliqué will be. The more roving you use, the denser the fabric and the more you will need to "stab" the two together. Even though you have taped the stencil, you may need to hold it in place with one hand while you're needle felting with the other.

3. Repeat

Add more roving to fill in the design as you move around the stencil, making sure you place the fiber exactly where you'd like it, changing colors as often or as little as you like.

Stab the roving repeatedly with the felting needle. Continue this process in all the open areas until the design is complete.

4. Wear it out

Dress up your baby and show off your style—both of you.

Beetle Juice!

Embroider with Shiny Beetle Wings

OVERVIEW

My design inspiration often comes from other disciplines. I was blown away when I came across Enrique Gomez de Molina's taxidermy sculptures at Spinello Gallery in Miami. He creates mystical creatures using representations and collected animal parts. One of his most captivating pieces is a rhino head covered in iridescent beetle wings. Relax, people, it's a rhino head carved from foam, and he collects the beetle wings after they are shed—no beetles are harmed in the process.

For weeks, I couldn't get the shimmery beetle wings out of my head, thinking they would make a dazzling accent to an outfit—a natural sequin, if you will. So, using a bold stencil, I came up with a technique for using beetle wings as sequins. You can apply them to any type of garment you like. Each wing already has a hole poked in it! Here's how I did it.

MATERIALS

- ○ **Garment of your choice** (I used a loose tank top)
- ○ **Stencil**
- ○ **Masking tape**
- ○ **Tailor's chalk** or **pencil**
- ○ **Beetle wings**
- ○ **Sewing needle**
- ○ **Thread**

Note: You can get the beetle wings online at www.ebay.com.

INSTRUCTIONS

1. Prep and position

Choose the garment you want to embellish and clear a flat work-space, like a table. Decide where you'd like the design to appear on the garment, and lay the fabric flat on your work surface. Place the stencil on the fabric and secure with masking tape.

2. Line the design

Trace the stencil pattern onto your garment using tailor's chalk or a pencil. Remove the stencil and fill in any lines that are too faint to follow.

3. Sew well

You will be sewing each beetle wing onto the garment inside the design area you outlined until all areas are filled. You want the beetle wings to hang toward the floor when you're wearing the garment.

Starting at the bottom-left space in the design, sew on one beetle wing. Then sew one next to it, beginning your first row. Continue across, left to right, until the space is filled. Then move up and begin the next row above your first wing, allowing some overlap. Continue attaching wings across until row two is complete. Repeat these steps until all the design areas are filled. It's a labor of love, and totally worth it!

4. Shimmer and shine

Once you've worked your fingers to the bone, you'll be ready for a night on the town with the other fairy godmothers and goddesses. Just say the magic words, and you're there.

Helmet Head

Spray-Paint a Bike Helmet

OVERVIEW

One of the first things I ever stenciled with my own design was my bike helmet. I spray-painted a chartreuse chimp head onto an army-green bike helmet. It made riding the streets of Brooklyn so much more fun. It's a fairly easy process, so let's get rolling!

MATERIALS

○ Helmet
○ Spray adhesive
○ Stencil
○ Scrap paper for overspray
○ Masking tape
○ Spray paint

Note: The helmet I used has a flat, matte surface with no graphics, which is ideal for this project. If your helmet has decals or lots of grooves and vents, you may need to employ patience (and a little sandpaper).

INSTRUCTIONS

1. Clean and prep

Start by making sure the surface of your helmet is free of dirt and dust by cleaning it with a damp cloth. Let it dry completely.

Apply some spray adhesive to the back of the stencil and let it dry 30 to 60 seconds, until tacky. Place the stencil where you'd like your design to appear. If it is on a very curvy part of the helmet, you may have to paint in sections. Use scrap paper and masking tape to mask off all areas outside the stencil where you do not want overspray to appear. If you like the overspray, don't mask!

2. Spray away

Holding the paint can 8 to 12 in/ 20 to 30 cm from the stencil, lightly spray in the open areas of the design. You can apply a second coat if you feel you have not filled in the design, but, again, it's better to go light and build up.

3. Reveal

Remove the stencil. Clean away any excess adhesive.

4. Ride it out

Once the paint is dry, put on your helmet and ride into the sunset!

Pretty Pooch

Make a One-of-a-Kind Doggie Tee

OVERVIEW

Dogs are second only to babies as the top living fashion accessory of the twenty-first century. So make sure you and your pup strut the streets in style by creating a customized tee just for his or her majesty. You don't have to spend a lot for your precious pooch to look like a million bucks.

MATERIALS

- ○ **Plain dog T-shirt**
- ○ **Fabric cream paint** or **Stencil1 Sprayers**
- ○ **Cardboard, shipping box**, or **shirt box**
- ○ **Stencil**
- ○ **Stencil spray adhesive** or **pushpins**
- ○ **Stencil brushes, foam brushes**, or **pouncer foam brushes**
- ○ **Safety goggles** (if spray-painting)
- ○ **Thick paper, cardboard**, or **poster board** to control overspray (if spray-painting)
- ○ **Iron** or **hair dryer**

Note: Plain doggie tees can be found online or at your local pet supply store.

1. Choose your doggie tee

Prewashed or preshrunk 100 percent cotton T-shirts work best. Polyester blends (50/50) yield mixed results, since they don't absorb the paint as easily. It is best to experiment first or to avoid them.

2. Choose your fabric paint

You'll find fabric paints at art supply stores. They require no mixing, have a thick consistency, are rich in pigmentation, and give long-lasting results. They even stand up to washing and drying. You can also use acrylic paint mixed with fabric medium (also available at art or craft supply stores) in a 1:1 ratio. Make sure the mixture is well blended. Stencil1 also has a line of multi-surface sprays. Stencil1 Sprayers are ideal for fabric. For a rougher look, you can use traditional spray paint, but with no guaranteed results.

3. Prepare your doggie tee

Place a piece of rectangular cardboard, a shipping box, or a shirt box inside the T-shirt to prevent paint from seeping through to the back of the doggie tee. This will also provide a flat surface to paint on. Depending on the size of your dog and its shirt, you may need only a small piece of cardboard. Make sure you don't stretch the shirt too much. Too much stretching will "warp" your design once it is taken off the box.

4. Position the stencil

Place the stencil on the doggie tee where you'd like the image to appear. Secure the stencil firmly in place using spray adhesive or pushpins. If you use spray adhesive, apply a light layer of adhesive to the back of the stencil. Allow the adhesive to dry until the surface becomes tacky, and then position your stencil.

5. Begin painting

You can use stencil brushes, foam brushes, or Stencil1 Sprayers to apply paint. If using a brush, do not overload it with paint. Too much paint on the brush causes the paint to seep under the edges of the stencil and creates blotchy designs. Remember—stenciling is a dry-brush technique. The most common mistake is overloading your brush. It is far better to build up the color gradually, layer by layer, instead of using one thick paint application. If paint begins to seep behind your stencil or if your designs do not have crisp, defined edges, you may be using too much paint.

Simply tap or dab the loaded brush against the stencil openings. (I recommend practicing on paper before you begin on your doggie tee.)

If you're using any kind of spray paint, be sure to wear safety goggles. Once you have the stencil secured in place, cover the outer

areas of the stencil with thick paper so as not to spray outside the stencil. Then, spray several small, light sprays in the open areas of the stencil. Once all areas are filled, carefully remove the stencil from the shirt to see your design. Be careful to lift the stencil parallel to the work, so as not to let excess paint drip on your shirt.

6. Seal it

Heat press your doggie tee before finishing or using a second stencil. After the paint has dried, turn the shirt inside out and iron the painted area on high heat for 1 to 2 minutes. You can also blow-dry with a hair dryer for 1 to 2 minutes.

7. Clean up

Lay your stencil flat to dry, wiping off any heavy paint. Careful cleaning and drying of your stencil brushes will enable them to be used again and again. Wash all excess paint off the brushes with warm running water and soap. Dry the brushes thoroughly before reuse.

8. Run with the big dogs

Show off your stylin' tee at the park, doggie day care, and your favorite fire hydrant.

Press Repeat

Use Repeat Patterns to Make a Stylish Skirt

OVERVIEW

Textile design is my dream job. Just as with stencil design, textile design is a collaboration. Someone designs the fabric, and another designer creates something with the fabric. Now you, too, can be a textile designer, and I'll show you how to make your own patterned fabric to use for clothing—in this case, a skirt.

MATERIALS

- Stencil1 Sprayers or fabric paint
- Cup or bowl
- Roll of solid-colored cotton fabric of your choice
- Stencil
- Stencil brush*
- Paper towels
- Scrap paper to control overspray (if spray-painting)*
- Blue painter's tape
- Garment pencil
- Ruler
- Spray Adhesive
- Iron

*optional

Note: I am using a soft cotton jersey for my fabric.

INSTRUCTIONS

1. Test

Pour spray ink or fabric paint into a cup or bowl. Cut a piece of test fabric. All fabric has different absorbency levels, so you have to see how the ink performs on the fabric you chose. Place the stencil on the fabric and, using a large stencil brush, dip the brush in the ink. Dry most of it off on a paper towel, and then apply the ink inside the open areas of the stencil in a pouncing motion. If you prefer to use the spray method, mask around the outside areas of the stencil with scrap paper and tape to prevent spray paint from getting under the paper. Lift your stencil and see how you did. If the ink bled into the fabric, you need to use less ink or paint. If all is well, time to move on to the real deal.

2. Prep

Lay out your fabric on a large, flat surface. Be sure you have enough space to work.

3. Plan

Plan your design. Figure out the repeating pattern you'd like to create. Make a grid on the material using a garment pencil and a ruler. This will mark the placement of the stencil for each row. Here are some ideas: You can have one stencil image repeat over and over, or alternate between two or three designs (bunny, tree, bunny, tree, etc.). You can also switch between colors (turquoise, red, turquoise, red, etc.). Go crazy. It's up to you and your imagination.

4. Paint

Place your stencil in the first space on your grid. I started with the top-left square. For a secure placement, spray the back of the stencil with a light coating of spray adhesive, allow to dry 30 to 60 seconds, then place the stencil on your fabric. If you're using Stencil1 Sprayers, mask the outer areas with scrap paper to avoid overspray. Paint in the open stencil areas as you did in the test piece (Step 1). Sprayers should be held 8 in/20 cm or so from the stencil. If brush-painting, carefully brush in the open areas of the stencil with very little paint. Once satisfied, lift the stencil carefully to avoid dripping. If any ink seeped to the back of the stencil, wipe it clean to avoid smudging.

Now, move to another place on your grid. Do this until the entire fabric is filled. Be careful to not smudge the area you just completed if you move to the very next space on the grid, especially if the stencil overlaps with what you just painted. To avoid this problem, you can just jump around the grid.

5. Press

Let the paint dry. Then heat seal the design with an iron. Set the iron on high with no steam, and press for 1 to 2 minutes in each painted area.

6. Create

Now, you can use your printed fabric to create clothing. Many skirt patterns can be found online to show you how to cut up your custom textile and sew it back together. In this case, we made a skirt. What will you make?

RESOURCES

STENCILS

This book!
Stencil 101
Stencil 101 Decor
Stencil 201
Stencil1.com—hundreds of designs!
Make your own!

ART SUPPLY STORES

Always support your local mom-and-pop art supply stores!

Then there are the big boys:
Aaron Brothers
A.C. Moore
Blick Art Materials
Flax Art & Design
Jo-Ann Fabric & Craft Stores
Michaels
Pearl Paint
Utrecht

BOOKS

STENCIL GRAFFITI

Banksy, *Wall and Piece*. London: Random House UK, 2007.

Cooper, Martha, and Henry Chalfant. *Subway Art: 25th Anniversary Edition*. San Francisco: Chronicle Books, 2009.

Fairey, Shepard. *Obey: Supply & Demand: The Art of Shepard Fairey*. 20th anniversary ed. Berkeley, CA: Gingko Press, 2009.

Ganz, Nicholas. *Graffiti World: Street Art from Five Continents*. 2nd ed. New York: Abrams, 2009.

Longhi, Samantha. *Stencil History X.*, c215, 2007.

MacPhee, Josh. *Stencil Pirates*. Berkeley, CA: Soft Skull Press, 2004.

Manco, Tristan. *Stencil Graffiti*. New York: Thames & Hudson, 2002.

Smallman, Jake, and Carl Nyman. *Stencil Graffiti Capital: Melbourne*. New York: Mark Batty Publisher, 2005.

HOW-TO AND INSPIRING ARTISTRY

Fagerstrom, Derek, and Lauren Smith. *Wallpaper Projects: 50 Craft and Design Ideas for Your Home, from Accents to Art*. San Francisco: Chronicle Books, 2009.

Hart, Jenny. *Embroidered Effects: Projects and Patterns to Inspire Your Stitching*. San Francisco: Chronicle Books, 2009.

Hughes, Ann d'Arcy, and Hebe Vernon-Morris. *The Printmaking Bible: The Complete Guide to Materials and Techniques*. San Francisco: Chronicle Books, 2008.

Innes, Jocasta. *Paint Magic*. 2nd ed. New York: Pantheon, 1989.

Moyle, Sabrina, and Eunice Moyle. *Handmade Hellos: Fresh Greeting Card Projects from First-Rate Crafters*. San Francisco: Chronicle Books, 2008.

Peot, Margaret. *Make Your Mark: Explore Your Creativity and Discover Your Inner Artist*. San Francisco: Chronicle Books, 2004.

Riva, Lesley, and Benjamin Moore Paints. *Paint Style: The New Approach to Decorative Paint Finishes*. Buffalo, NY: Firefly Books, 2008.

Terry, Kayte. *Appliqué Your Way*. San Francisco: Chronicle Books, 2009.

T-SHIRTS

Thrift and recycled-clothing stores (the best places for one-of-kind fashion on a budget)

Alternative Apparel (great vintage-style T-shirts and variety of cuts)

American Apparel (a wide variety of cuts, fabrics, and colors)

WEB SITES

Stencil1.com
See our designs in a variety of sizes, plus our full product line. View stenciled items in our gallery, watch our video tutorials, and send in your Stencil1 project images.

Etsy.com
This marketplace of handmade and vintage wares inspires and promotes artists everywhere.

Graffiti.org
Art Crimes is a gallery of graffiti art from the United States, Europe, and cities around the world.

WoosterCollective.com
The Wooster Collective was founded in 2001. This site is dedicated to showcasing and celebrating ephemeral art placed on streets in cities around the world.

YouTube.com
Search YouTube for lots of great "how-to stencil" videos.

MORE INTERNET INSPIRATION

ApartmentTherapy.com
Craftster.org
CraftStylish.com
Craftzine.com
CutOutAndKeep.net
DesignSponge.com
DIYnetwork.com
Flickr.com (search for "stencil art")
Instructables.com
Makezine.com
Readymade.com
Selvedge.org
ThreadBanger.com
Threadless.com
ThreadsMagazine.com
UnanimousCraft.com

BLOGS

Stencil1.com/news
Apair-andaspare.blogspot.com
AshleyRoseHelvey.blogspot.com
Blog.fashiolista.com
CoolHunting.com
CraftCritique.com
CraftGossip.com
CraftyPod.com
DesignSpongeOnline.com
GlitterNGlue.com
JustSomethingIMade.blogspot.com
Outsapop.com
StencilHistoryX.com
Studs-and-Pearls.com
UnnecessaryUmlaut.com

ACKNOWLEDGMENTS

I'd like to thank all of the talented guests in the book for their inspiration and for showing us fashionable and new ways to work with stencils. Also, thanks to the creative people who surround me in my life, both friends and idols—you inspire and influence my own work. To Leigh Angel, who crafts, writes, and sends joy my way, thank you for your help with this book. Thanks to my publishing family at Chronicle Books and to YOU—thanks for believing in Stencil1 and making things with my stencils!

Stencil 1® © Copyright Ed Roth

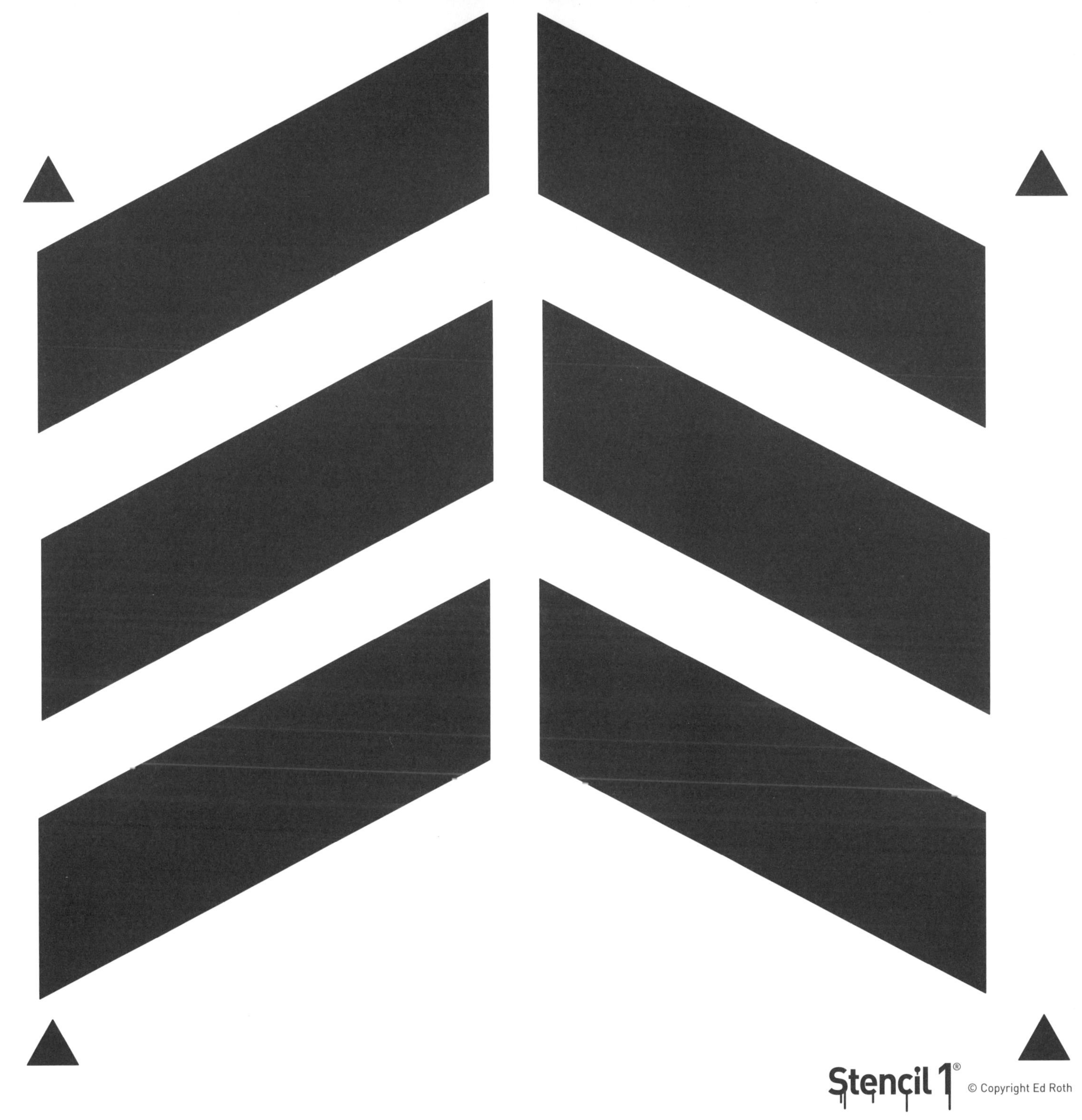
Stencil 1®
© Copyright Ed Roth

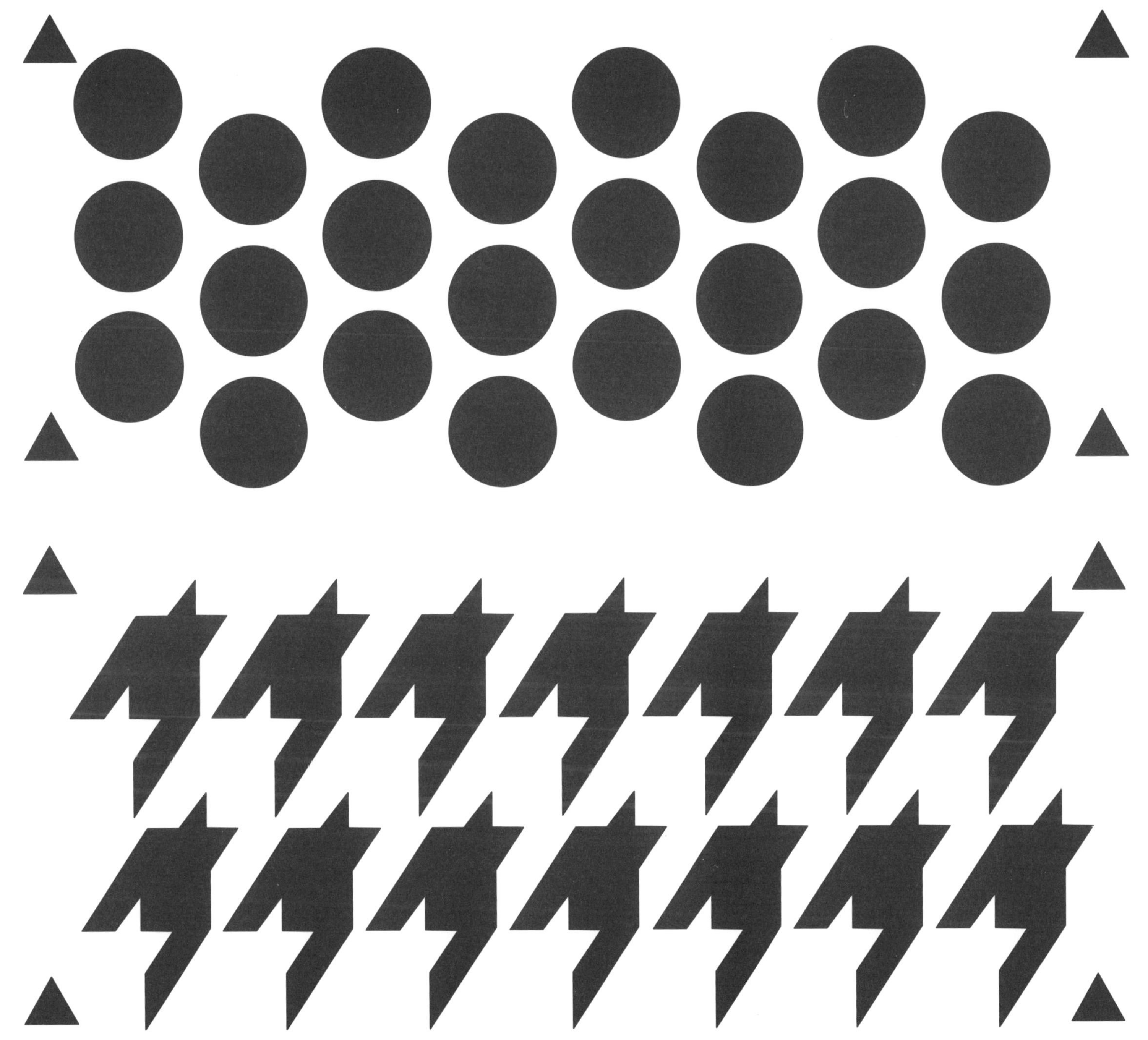

Stencil 1
© Copyright Ed Roth

Stencil 1®
© Copyright Ed Roth

Stencil 1
© Copyright Ed Roth

Stencil1®
© Copyright Ed Roth

Stencil1
© Copyright Ed Roth

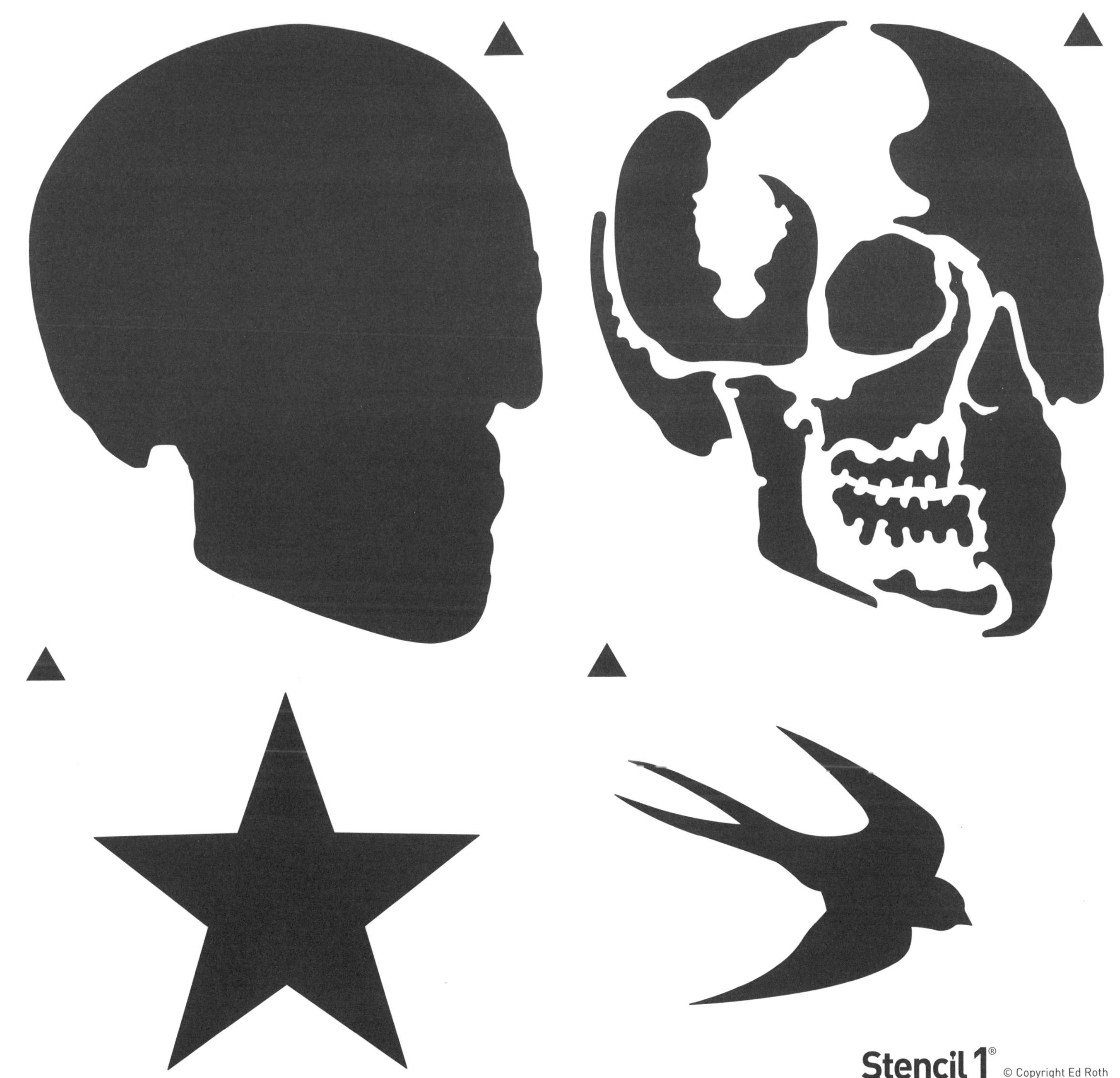
Stencil 1®
© Copyright Ed Roth

Stencil 1
© Copyright Ed Roth

Stencil1®
© Copyright Ed Roth

Stencil1®
© Copyright Ed Roth

Stencil 1®
© Copyright Ed Roth

Stencil 1®
© Copyright Ed Roth

Stencil1®

BROOKLYN

EV
OL
VE

NEW YORK
PARIS
LONDON
HONG KONG
MILAN
BROOKLYN

A B C D E F G
H I J K L M N
O P Q R S T U
V W X Y Z 1 2
3 4 5 6 7 8 9 0